New Directions in Italian and Italian-American History

Selected Essays from the Conference in Honor of Dr. Philip Cannistraro

EDITED BY

Ernest Ialongo

William M. Adams

JOHN D. CALANDRA ITALIAN AMERICAN INSTITUTE
QUEENS COLLEGE, CITY UNIVERSITY OF NEW YORK

STUDIES IN ITALIAN AMERICANA
VOLUME 6

John D. Calandra Italian American Institute
Queens College, CUNY
25 West 43rd Street, 17th floor
New York, NY 10036

ISBN 0-9703403-9-7
ISBN 978-0-9703403-9-9
Library of Congress Control Number: 2012924066

This volume is dedicated to
the late Dr. Philip V. Cannistraro

TABLE OF CONTENTS

ACKNOWLEDGEMENTS

In putting together the conference, "New Directions in Italian and Italian American History," as well as in preparing this volume, Ernest Ialongo and Bill Adams received much help and encouragement along the way. Drs. Mary Gibson and Marta Petrusewicz provided the idea of a conference that would honor the legacy of Philip Cannistraro, one in which his former graduate students should have a prominent place. Marcella Bencivenni, Peter Vellon and David Aliano deserve special thanks for their early efforts and continuing support through the process. The chairs and presenters at the conference (detailed in the "Introduction" to this volume) also deserve a special thanks. They all contributed greatly to the success of the conference, and many came from a great distance to take part in the event.

Financial support was integral to the conference and specific organizations came through with much needed help in financially straightened times. The Office of Academic Affairs at Hostos Community College, CUNY, the Ph.D. Program in History at the CUNY Graduate School, and the History Department at Queens College, CUNY, all provided some form of financial support. Respectively, we would like to acknowledge Provost Carmen Coballes-Vega and Dean Christine Mangino of Hostos Community College, Dr. Helena Rosenblatt of the Ph.D. Program in History at the CUNY Graduate School, and Dr. Frank Warren of the History Department at Queens College for their help. There was one anonymous donor to the conference who came through with much needed financing at the last moment. This person insists on remaining anonymous, but we hope that acknowledging this person's contribution here in this volume will stand as but a small token of our gratitude.

Finally, and most especially, Ialongo and Adams would like to thank Anthony Julian Tamburri, Dean of the John D. Calandra Italian American Institute. Dean Tamburri not only offered his Institute to host the conference, but provided solid financial and logistical support, and graciously met with the organizers on many occasions to work out the details. He also supported the publication of the proceedings, which this volume represents. The conference would simply not have happened without

Dean Tamburri's involvement, and it is impossible to list the many ways he made the conference and this volume possible. To him our deepest thanks.

Dr. Ernest Ialongo and Dr. William M. Adams

New Directions in Italian and Italian American History

Ernest Ialongo and William M. Adams

On November 5, 2011 the John D. Calandra Italian American Institute hosted a conference entitled "New Directions in Italian and Italian American History: A Conference in Honor of Philip Cannistraro." Cannistraro was many things to many people: friend, mentor, partner, teacher, and relentless advocate to get on with your work. In his all too abbreviated life, his work managed to revolutionize both the fields of Italian history and Italian American history, and set in motion a future generation of scholars who would take up many of the questions he began raising so many years ago and, in turn, would demand answers using the same rigorous methodology that characterized his own work. When Cannistraro's life was cut tragically short in May 2005 after a courageous battle with cancer, the field of history lost a giant at the height of his intellectual powers. We lost a biography of Mussolini that remains incomplete, we lost a planned biography of Generoso Pope, and we lost the possibility of his landmark book *La fabbrica del consenso* being translated into English with an introduction that would have critically examined the field of Fascist cultural studies and highlighted questions still left unanswered. We lost future journal articles and insightful book reviews, inspiring lectures and critical expertise. We lost much.

Philip V. Cannistraro was born in the Bronx in 1942 and spent most of his life in and around the New York City area. He completed all three of his degrees at New York University, culminating with his Ph.D. in 1971 with a dissertation on mass media and culture in Fascist Italy, which would be published in Italian as *La fabbrica del consenso: Fascismo e mass media* in 1975 with a preface by the esteemed Italian historian of Fascism Renzo De Felice.[1] He then took up a position as Assistant Professor of History at Florida State University immediately upon graduation and remained there until 1982, achieving the rank of Full Professor, and serving as Associate Chair of the History Department for a time. Thereafter,

---

[1] Philip Cannistraro, *La fabbrica del consenso: Fascismo e mass media* (Rome: Laterza, 1975).

he was Professor of History at Drexel University in Philadelphia from 1982 to 1995, and served as the Chair of the Department of History and Politics for five of those years. In 1996 Cannistraro made his way back to his hometown and took up the position of Distinguished Professor of Italian American Studies with a joint posting at Queens College and the Graduate School of the City University of New York. At the latter institution Cannistraro was integral in forming the Italian History section of the Ph.D. Program in History. Another honor achieved at CUNY was the position of Acting Executive Director of the John D. Calandra Italian American Institute from 2000 to 2003.

The list of Cannistraro's scholarly work is vast, and much of it has had notable influence in the fields of both Italian and Italian-American history. In addition to the groundbreaking *La fabbrica del consenso*, which Emilio Gentile discusses at length in his contribution to our present volume, we must also point to the biography he co-authored with Brian R. Sullivan of Mussolini's lover, *Il Duce's Other Woman: The Untold Story of Margherita Sarfatti* (1993). More than a biography, this work is a primer on the cultural battles between modernists and conservatives in Fascist Italy, and gives a clear reckoning of the growth of anti-Semitism in the regime and its effect on Sarfatti and other Italian Jews.[2] He also performed a signal pedagogical service by editing *Fascist Italy: An Historical Dictionary* (1982), which made available a hitherto inaccessible breadth of data to many scholars working on the history of Fascism.[3] Cannistraro also contributed greatly to the world of Italian-American history. His edited volume of proceedings from the conference of the same name, *Italian Americans: The Search for a Usable Past* (1989), is a testament to his desire to push for a more rigorous investigation of Italian-American history.[4] His *Blackshirts in Little Italy* (1999) gives a thorough account, based on archival sources, of how the Fascist regime attempted to establish a global network across the Italian diaspora.[5] He moved the field of Italian-American history into a more public realm, beyond the world of scholarship, when

---

[2] Philip Cannistraro and Brian R. Sullivan, *Il Duce's Other Woman: The Untold Story of Margherita Sarfatti* (New York: William Morrow, 1993).

[3] Philip Cannistraro, ed., *Fascist Italy: An Historical Dictionary* (Westport, CT: Greenwood Press, 1982).

[4] Philip Cannistraro and Richard Juliani, eds., *Italian Americans: The Search for a Usable Past* (New York: Proceeding of the American Italian Historical Association, 1989).

[5] Philip Cannistraro, *Blackshirts in Little Italy: Italian Americans and Fascism, 1920-1929* (Lafayette, IN: Bordighera, 1999).

he curated an exhibition at the New-York Historical Society, *The Italians of New York* (1999), the first museum exhibition in New York City on the Italian-American experience. He edited the catalog for this exhibition and wrote its introduction.[6] What might be seen as the crowning achievement of his work in Italian-American history was the conference and subsequent book *The Lost World of Italian American Radicalism* (2003)—co-edited, and with an extensive introduction co-written with Gerald Meyer—which brought the study of Italian-American radicalism into the mainstream of historical study.[7]

This was Cannistraro's legacy: to force new questions and lines of research in his two fields. In 2009 a group of Cannistraro's last graduate students came together to discuss the possibility of holding a conference to honor their departed mentor and to pay tribute to his legacy. The idea originated with fellow Italianists Drs. Mary Gibson and Marta Petrusewicz of the Graduate School of the City University of New York. After meeting together on several occasions, these (now former) graduate students, Ernest Ialongo, Bill Adams, Marcella Bencivenni, David Aliano and Peter Vellon decided to host a formal conference to which former students and established scholars who had worked with or been influenced by Cannistraro would be invited to contribute to a discussion on "New Directions in Italian and Italian American History." It was at this point that Dean Anthony Tamburri of the John D. Calandra Italian American Institute stepped into the picture. He worked closely with the chief organizers of the conference, Ernest Ialongo and Bill Adams, and generously provided much-needed financing and expert advice to a couple of novice conference organizers.

Emilio Gentile, who had worked with Cannistraro since the mid-1970s in the field of Fascist studies, agreed to be the keynote speaker and introduced the conference with an address that expertly detailed the nature of Cannistraro's influence on Fascist historiography over three decades. Three sessions followed the keynote address: one for Italian American history, and two for Italian history. Gerald Meyer chaired the Italian American panel, consisting of Charles Killinger, Peter Vellon, and Marcella Bencivenni. Emily Braun led the first panel on Italian history, consist-

---

[6] Philip Cannistraro, ed., *The Italians of New York,* exhibition catalog (New York: The New-York Historical Society, 1999).

[7] Philip Cannistraro and Gerald Meyer, eds., *The Lost World of Italian American Radicalism* (Westport, CT: Praeger, 2003).

ing of Paul Corner, Ernest Ialongo and Bill Adams; and John Davis headed the second, which included Marta Petrusewicz, Stanislao Pugliese and David Aliano. The panels ranged widely in their topics, but all held true to the mandate that the presenters should bring to the conference a representation of innovative work in either Italian or Italian-American history. Thus, Killinger gave a précis of his recent work on Renato Poggioli, Vellon discussed his forthcoming book on race and Italian-Americans, and Bencivenni investigated the culture of Italian-American radicals. Corner shared his critical appraisal of the concept of consensus in the Fascist regime, and Ialongo and Adams addressed the topic of intellectuals under Fascism—Ialongo focusing on the Futurist Filippo Tommaso Marinetti, and Adams on the press during the Republic of Salò. In the final session, Petrusewicz discussed her recent work on nineteenth-century Rome, Pugliese presented some of the findings of his new work on the history of Naples, and Aliano explored the links between the Fascist regime and the Italian community in Argentina. All of this work had either been recently published, or was about to find its way to publication.

With the success of the conference, the next step was to compile a volume commemorating the event. What follows in this volume is a series of papers collected from all who were able to contribute, some entirely new, some in the same form they were delivered at the conference with the requisite references added. The editors respected as much as possible the integrity of the drafts submitted and, other than standardizing the formatting and references, kept their emendations limited to spelling and grammatical errors. The order of presentation is meant to trace evolving themes that emerged as the papers were read in their entirety, and the reader may perhaps benefit from reading them in that order. Gentile's keynote address was translated by Ialongo and is reprinted in its entirety. Gentile's discussion of the influence of *La fabbrica del consenso* and the problems both Cannistraro and he faced as historians as they examined the topic of consensus within the Fascist regime is followed by Corner's paper, which further investigates the validity of the concept of consensus in a dictatorship. Ialongo's paper continues the focus on Fascism, concentrating on how Marinetti decisively shaped a key ingredient of the Fascist propaganda machine: the myth of the Duce as the all-knowing and "good" leader. Ialongo also shows how Marinetti sought to define the Duce's image as both modern and revolutionary, and how this was meant to benefit his Futurist movement in the cut-throat cultural battles of Fascist Italy. Adams's paper follows, with a continuing focus on intellectuals and Fascism, this time during the final phase of Fascism under the Salò Republic, exploring the way Mussolini connived with key newspaper editors to foster the illusion that a renovated Fascism would embrace public debate. Pugliese's paper on Ignazio Silone, which also contributes to the discussion of the intellectual's role under Fascism, tackles the thorny issue of Silone's alleged collaboration with Mussolini's government, a regime radically antagonistic to the leftist politics associated with this writer. Killinger's paper follows, offering a bridge between Italian and Italian-American history. Killinger investigates the lives of anti-Fascist intellectuals Renato Poggioli and Gaetano Salvemini as they escaped Fascism for America, and then sought to make their way in both mainstream America and the Italian-American community. Meyer's paper continues the study of Italian-Americans with an overview of the plight of this population during the Great Depression and how this experience deepened political activism connected to the New Deal Left and other, even further leftist, organizations—a conclusion that departs significantly from the traditional view of Italian-Americans as insular "amoral familists." Finally, Bencivenni's paper anchors our volume, presenting a discussion of the radicalism of the Italian immigrants in the early twentieth century. She focuses principally on immigrants' mobilization of culture as a means of spreading various leftist ideas, blending anti-Fascism with anti-capitalism, and how their efforts laid the basis for the later activism Meyer's paper discusses.

We hope with this volume to show our readers how Philip Cannistraro's work continues to have a deep and lasting impact in both Italian history and Italian American history. It is but a brief sampling of the promising work that is being done in these fields today, which in many ways is indebted to the pioneering work and relentless energy of our sorely missed friend and mentor.

FABBRICA DEL CONSENSO O FABBRICA DEL POTERE?
REDEFINING FASCISM AND TOTALITARIANISM

Emilio Gentile
(Translated by Ernest Ialongo)

It is a great pleasure for me to have been invited to give the keynote address at this conference in honor of Philip Cannistraro. Ten years ago, when I invited Phil to offer a course at the University of Rome on the role of Italian-Americans in the history of the United States, I introduced him to my students as one of those historians who, in the course of the Seventies, had significantly contributed to putting the study of Fascism on a new research basis, one no longer influenced by ideological polemics. Of course, Phil was not simply conducting neutral research either, devoid of any principles or values. And, to clarify my point, I quoted a passage written by Phil for Gaetano Salvemini's book, *Italian Fascist Activities in the United States*, which Phil had edited in 1977. "Salvemini," he wrote, "left a rich legacy for later generations, and surely one bequest of value is the lesson that if Fascism must be studied and understood with reason and [the] logic of the mind, it should also be fought with the instincts and passions of the soul."[1]

I think these words could be used to describe Phil's historical work, and his legacy as an historian of Fascism, Antifascism, and Italian-Americans. In his work, Phil always brought together thorough research in the public and private archives with his unique sensibility as a man and as an historian in order to discover the concrete experiences of the men and women of both Fascism and Antifascism. Possibly, this sensibility was responsible for his preference for biography, a type of writing that immerses the historian in the real life of their subject, and through that subject's life one tries to better understand a particular cultural or political movement. I want to highlight that Phil's personal and intellectual curiosity was not simply concerned with the lives of the famous, such as

---

[1] G. Salvemini, *Italian Fascist Activities in the United States*, edited with an introduction by Philip V. Cannistraro (New York: Center for Migration Studies, 1977), xl.

Margherita Sarfatti and Benito Mussolini, but it also explored the minor personages that history had forgotten, such as the socialist Maria Giudice, friend of Angelica Balabanoff, who Phil rescued from oblivion with one of his final articles, "Who was Angelica Balabanoff's 'Maria'? A Note on Historical Identification," published in 2003.[2] Phil's comments in the conclusion of his article on Maria Giudice illustrate the fundamental humanism of his historical interests:

> Giudice's career as a socialist militant stretched over the course of almost half a century. During that time, she held positions that ranged from local prominence to national importance, and her work brought her into contact with major figures in Italian socialism, from Angelica Balabanoff and Antonio Gramsci to Benito Mussolini and Pietro Nenni. Giudice was not of their intellectual stature or international renown. Rather, her importance lies in the extraordinarily consistent life of sacrifice and struggle that she led in the cause of socialist revolution. The very fact that she has been virtually forgotten speaks to the common experience of an entire generation of rank-and-file figures in Italian Marxism whom history has largely ignored but whose contributions made it such a rich and powerful movement.[3]

If his human sensibility and his cultural and political formation had rendered Phil sympathetic to the personages of Antifascism, his aversion to Fascism did not impede him from studying even this phenomenon "with reason and [the] logic of the mind." And Phil engaged in this endeavor by confronting one of the most complicated and most controversial aspects of Fascism: its relationship to culture, the masses, and the politics of consensus. In my talk today, I would like to discuss some of Phil's conclusions on the cultural politics of Fascism and more generally on totalitarian Fascism, which were the subjects of our conversations in the last five years of his life. As such, I am not only honored to have been invited to introduce this conference in honor of Phil, but I am in debt to the organizers because they have given me the opportunity to publicly take up again a conversation with Phil which, for me, intellectually, has never been interrupted in the years since his passing.

---

[2] P.V. Cannistraro, "Who Was Angelica Balabanoff's 'Maria'? A Note on Historical Identification," *Science & Society* 67. 3 (Fall 2003), 349-352.
[3] Ibid., 352.

My conversation with Phil began nearly forty years ago, in 1975, when, in an unexpected coincidence, our books were published within a few months of each other and by the same press: my *Le origini dell'ideologia fascista* and Phil's *La fabbrica del consenso*.[4] I'm pleasantly reminded at this point that Phil encouraged the translation of my book into English, and was reading over chapters of the translation while he was already ill. He had also offered to write a preface to the translation, but was already too ill to complete the task.

In 1975 I did not know Cannistraro personally. I had only read his article "Mussolini's Cultural Revolution: Fascist or Nationalist?" published in 1972, and I did not agree with what he wrote in the conclusion: "In the final analysis, . . . Mussolini's cultural revolution represented the successful absorption and reshaping of nationalist ideology into the rhetorical framework of Fascism."[5] And, I was not in agreement with various conclusions Cannistraro put forward in *La fabbrica del consenso*. In spite of this, I wrote in a brief review that I considered his book to be one of the best studies ever done on Fascist cultural politics. At that time, there were so few studies on this period, and not all of them were historically sound.

It is important to remember, especially for the younger historians, that when Cannistraro began his research at the end of the Sixties on the cultural politics of Fascism most historians of Fascism were justly convinced that "it should be fought with the instincts and passions of the soul," but few historians pushed themselves to also understand Fascism "with reason and [the] logic of the mind." As such, the majority of historians of all ideological persuasions considered Fascism as a phenomenon without ideology, without culture, and ultimately without its own original political system. And those that did not share this conviction ran the risk of being accused of being apologists for Fascism.

Being aware of the state of Fascist studies at the beginning of the Seventies, it is possible to better understand the originality and the importance of Phil's book on the cultural politics of Fascism, and the historiographical effect it had both in Italy and internationally. As Renzo De

---

[4] P.V. Cannistraro, *La fabbrica del consenso. Fascismo e mass media*, prefazione di R. De Felice (Roma-Bari: Laterza, 1975); E. Gentile, *Le origini dell'ideologia fascista (1918-1925)* (Roma-Bari: Laterza, 1975), translated as *The Origins of Fascist Ideology (1918-1925)*, translated by R. Miller (New York: Enigma Books, 2006).
[5] P. V. Cannistraro, "Mussolini's Cultural Revolution: Fascist or Nationalist?," *Journal of Contemporary History* 7.3/4 (July-October 1972), 115-139.

Felice noted in the preface to *La fabbrica del consenso*, it was already commonplace in Italy at that time "to lament the dearth of studies, of adequate analyses, on the cultural politics of Fascism and the relations between Fascism and the intellectuals," but at the same time, added De Felice, "as if to fill this void, it is asked if a Fascist culture existed at all, if Fascism had any culture at all, and if nationalism had imposed its hegemony on Fascism or vice versa, etc." In such a situation, continued De Felice, "we don't believe we are exaggerating when we state that this is an important book by Philip Cannistraro, [and] that [it] can exercise a positive influence for quite some time on Fascist studies. . . ."[6]

The principal merit that De Felice attributed to Cannistraro's book, in addition to it being based on vast, unpublished documents, and to the originality of the themes it dealt with, was to "have confronted in modern, and we believe, convincing terms the problem of trying to concretely understand 'mass culture' in a regime such as the Fascist one." Another of Cannistraro's merits, according to De Felice, was having avoided "trying to fit the Italian situation into a Procrustean bed of a typology, of a model totalitarianism, which tends to be distortive and ultimately false, and that, in every case, makes it practically impossible to deal with a whole series of decisive issues."

This final consideration by De Felice, with its very critical judgment on "model totalitarianism," ignored, I believe, an important question that Cannistraro had raised both in the introduction as well as in various conclusions expressed in his book, and this specifically dealt with the concept of totalitarian Fascism. On this question, De Felice himself had expressed uncertain and contradictory conclusions, as I've demonstrated elsewhere.[7] In those years, in fact, in both Italian and foreign historiography, what dominated was not only the vision of Fascism as a movement without ideology and culture, but generally the conviction—based on the work of Hannah Arendt—that Fascism was not a totalitarian phenomenon at all, but a common nationalist dictatorship, that had a variety of criminal characteristics, but was ultimately a dictatorship that was more good-natured than cruel, more scoundrel than tragic. This representation of the Fascist regime was also a consequence of an attempt at the "defascitization of Fascism," as I've defined it, prevalent in the press and in Ital-

---

[6] R. De Felice, preface to Cannistraro, *La fabbrica del consenso*, ix.
[7] E. Gentile, *Renzo De Felice. Lo storico e il personaggio* (Rome-Bari: Laterza, 2003).

ian historiography after 1945.[8] This attempt, mostly favored by the neo-fascist and conservative press, but also taken up by a part of the left wing press, consisted in denying to Fascism the attributes that were historically inherent to it as a new experiment in political domination, put in place by an armed party that assumed a monopoly of power and politics through force, and imposed on the Italians a one-party regime, a dogmatic ideology, the cult of the leader, and the permanent mobilization of the population—all regimented in a capillary mass organization.[9] It is important to point out here that it was these very aspects of the lived reality of Fascism that led the Antifascists to coin a new word at the end of the Twenties, "totalitarianism," in order to define the nature and originality of the Fascist experiment in political domination. And to be more precise, in using the term "totalitarianism" to define Fascism, the Antifascists were not only referring to its intentions, its ambitions and to its aspirations, but were also referring to its reality, that is, its organization as an armed party, its concrete actions to conquer and impose its monopoly of power and political control, and they were referring to its methods of control which were used to force the population to submit through ideological and cultural means.[10]

The prevalence of the "defascitization of Fascism" in the historiography as well as in the press had precluded for nearly three decades, until the middle of the Seventies, the possibility of studying and understanding the nature, the significance and the function of the institutions and methods characteristic of Fascist totalitarianism, including the activities of the intellectuals and the uses of culture, which, instead, had been objects of close analysis mostly on the part of various Antifascist scholars, such as Luigi Sturzo, Carlo Rosselli, Gaetano Salvemini, Antonio Gramsci and Palmiro Togliatti. And it was the "rediscovery" of these studies of totalitarian Fascism by the Antifascists during the Seventies that triggered an extended process of research and reflection—above all represented by Cannistraro's work — that led to a redefinition of Fascism through a redefinition of totalitarianism, and has produced in the last decades impressive progress in the study of the institutions and the organization of

---

[8] See E. Gentile, *Fascismo. Storia e interpretazione* (Roma-Bari: Laterza, 2002), v-xi.

[9] See E. Gentile, *La via italiana al totalitarismo. Partito e Stato nel regime fascista*, nuova edizione (Roma: Carocci, 2008), 341-354.

[10] See A. Gleason, *Totalitarianism. The Inner History of the Cold War* (New York-Oxford: Oxford University Press, 1995), 13-14; Gentile, *Fascismo*, 65-70.

Fascism, in addition to producing new and deeper studies on its ideology, its culture and its cultural politics.

I must personally recognize at this point that Cannistraro's book was also an important stimulus to the redefinition of Fascism and totalitarianism in my own work, even if I did not agree with all the solutions he proposed.

In the introduction to *La fabbrica del consenso*, Cannistraro expertly highlighted the many difficulties encountered in the study of the cultural history of Fascism, which were at the time, as he defined it: "virgin territory from the point of view of scientific inquiry." But the biggest problems derived from the totalitarian nature of Fascist domination. "In the case of Italy during the Fascist period—wrote Cannistraro—things were . . . complicated by the fact that each sector of cultural life was brought under the state's gaze and keenly influenced by the political and moral imperatives of the totalitarian state and the Fascist party. It follows that to understand the cultural experience of contemporary Italy it is essential to understand Fascism."[11]

Cannistraro was convinced that, in spite of the uncertainties and the oscillations in its cultural choices, "the regime developed a variety of basic constants that characterized its cultural politics." Among those constants were, as Cannistraro wrote, "the attempt to reach the total integration of the entire population in a unique national experience." Because of this, Cannistraro believed that Fascism was, in fact, and contrary to the prevailing ideas at the time, "a manifestation of the totalitarian phenomenon" and was "essentially a product of modern mass society." It was within a totalitarian state, he added, that Fascism was "a new and original system of government, whose success depended on the capacity to organize, inspire and control the lives of men, be it at the level of large social groups, or at the level of the individual." Consequently, he concluded, "in order to remain in power and realize its revolutionary aspirations, Fascism had to tie the mass of Italians to the regime, creating between the former and the latter a profound bond, and establishing a new level of national consciousness. The Fascists saw their major long- term objective to forge a nation in the totalitarian sense, which included the

---

[11] Cannistraro, *La fabbrica del consenso*, 3.

modernization of Italy and the integration of every socio-economic group in a common identity."[12]

One of the means of achieving this objective was the mass media, with which Fascism sought to realize what Cannistraro defined as another constant of Fascist cultural politics, that is, the attempt to destroy the class basis of Italian culture, bringing culture to the workers and the peasants and to society's other disadvantaged groups in order to end "the cultural monopoly retained by the middle and upper classes until that time," and to destroy the concept of the autonomy of the intellectuals in order to constrain them to serve the social and political interests of Fascism. "Even if in this attempt—Cannistraro continued—the regime suffered one of its most obvious failures, the objective had a central place in its cultural politics," which, even if "tormented by internal contradictions and exhaustive implications, it was incontestably a part of the regime."[13] As such, Cannistraro meant to study "Fascist cultural politics in and of themselves" in order to "explain the nature of its choices and the general cultural values of Italian Fascism when transformed into a regime."[14]

> Such an approach—explained Cannistraro—implies, in fact demands, that we investigate our subject 'from within' and from the perspective that it is necessary to the historical inquiry. It goes without saying that no historian can be 'objective' in an absolutely pure way, as the selection and classification of data is a subjective process. In the final analysis, everyone undoubtedly determines their historical conclusions—one cannot do any differently—on the basis of their moral values and their conscience. Still—Phil continued—it does not seem necessary, or wise, to write history explicitly proposing to either validate—or condemn—a particular political or economic philosophy. The nature of Fascism's 'political structure' naturally emerges from the total effect of Fascism, whether the author wants it or not. We accept, therefore, the judgment that Fascism was a corrupt and dehumanizing phenomenon, which we must avoid repeating; and, in order to impede its repetition, it is necessary to force oneself to understand its nature scrupulously and with an open mind.[15]

---

[12] Ibid., 6-8.
[13] Ibid., 9.
[14] Ibid., 5.
[15] Ibid., 4-5.

It is interesting to note here that the approach Cannistraro chose to study Fascist cultural politics corresponded to the approach George L. Mosse proposed in order to study Nazism, and that is through an effort at intellectual empathy: "As a trained historian,—explained Mosse in his autobiography—I have some practice in attempting to go back in time to see how people living then understood their world. I have always believed that empathy is the chief quality a historian needs to cultivate. . . . Empathy means putting contemporary prejudices aside while looking at the past without fear or favor." [16] "Empathy," he continued, "is still at the core of the historical enterprise for me, but understanding does not mean withholding judgment. I myself have mainly dealt with people and movements whom I judged harshly, but understanding must precede an informed and effective judgment."[17]

I wanted to quote Mosse's views along with Cannistraro's, because their views on how to study Fascist culture were the themes of my final conversations with Phil, which we had in March of 2001 in Rome, when he was teaching his course on Italian-Americans, and in October of the following year in London, on the occasion of a conference entitled "Culture, Censorship and the Italian State."

And there is another personal memory I have, which brings together in my mind my two friends. I'm referring to a conversation the three of us had in Chicago, in December 1991, during the American Historical Association conference. In Chicago, the topic of the conversation was my interpretation of Fascism as a totalitarian phenomenon, which implied a redefinition of both Fascism and totalitarianism, and consequently a reconsideration of the relations between Fascism and culture and, more generally, the problem of consensus in the Fascist regime, which both Mosse and Cannistraro placed at the center of their work. From both of them I received a critical push to continue my work on the Fascist party and the regime, specifically my work on what I was calling at that time—paraphrasing the title of Phil's book—la "fabbrica del potere," the factory of power.

However, although we agreed on *how* to study Fascism, in my conversations with Phil in Rome and in London we debated his conclusions

---

[16] G.L. Mosse, *Confronting History. A Memoir* (Madison: The University of Wisconsin Press, 2000), 5.

[17] Ibid., 172.

regarding Fascist cultural politics after 1936 in *La fabbrica del consenso*. "Taken altogether—Phil had written—the cultural themes of the final years of the Thirties—from the mythic liturgy of Romanità, to the inhuman degradation of anti-Semitism, to the utopian tensions towards the 'new man'—all represented the unrealistic and irrational extremism of a political culture in bankruptcy. They were the solutions of a desperate regime emptied of any internal vitality and coming to grips with the realization of its own failure."[18] I disagreed with Phil, since, at the beginning of 2000, I had just conducted thorough research on these Fascist themes, and the results of my research led me to a view of Fascism at the end of the Thirties quite different from that described by Phil in 1975.

I did not share his conclusions in *La fabbrica del consenso* because I believed—and I still believe, as I explained to Phil during our conversations—that the myth and liturgy of Romanità, the inhuman degradation of anti-Semitism, and the utopian tensions towards the new man were not an extreme and irrational reaction of a cultural politics in bankruptcy, nor the desperate solution of a regime close to failure, but were cultural themes coherent with the political culture of Fascism and with the totalitarian nature of its experiment in domination.[19] Many of these themes were present in Fascism at the beginning of the regime, and anti-Semitism, officially adopted in 1938, was itself a consequence of the intensifying totalitarian nature of Fascism which Mussolini wanted to imprint on the internal politics of the regime, even though he knew that this process, corresponding to the intensifying bellicosity in foreign policy, would surely provoke a crisis amongst the mass of Italians. In the end, this crisis, amply documented by police reports, did not keep the regime from following an ever more extreme internal politics, at a time in which, in reality, there was no internal force which questioned—much less threatened—the stability and existence of the regime.[20]

From these critical observations on Phil's conclusions on Fascist cultural politics in the late Thirties, our conversations then moved on to discuss the problem of consensus which was raised in a clear and decisive way in the title of his book *La fabbrica del consenso*. Today, I regret not having asked Phil if the title was chosen by him, by the publisher, or if it was

---

[18] Cannistraro, *La fabbrica del consenso*, 148.

[19] See E. Gentile, *Fascismo di pietra* (Roma-Bari: Laterza, 2007).

[20] See E. Gentile, *La Grande Italia, The Myth of the Nation in the Twentieth Century*, translated by S. Dingee and J. Pudney (Madison: The University of Wisconsin Press, 2009), 164 ff.

suggested by Renzo De Felice, who just the previous year had published a new volume of his biography of Mussolini, dedicated to the years 1929-1936, calling them "the years of consensus."[21] In any case, whoever was the inventor, the title was certainly suggestive and effective. It probably contributed to the success of the book and its author. "La fabbrica del consenso" has become a universally known and used expression in the study of Fascism, even if sometimes those that use it forget who introduced it into the historiography. However, beyond the efficacy of the expression, I always had concerns regarding the role and significance of the very notion of consensus in the study of Fascism as a totalitarian phenomenon—a concern Phil and I shared.

The first reason for my doubts on the idea of consensus in the study of Fascism had to do with the possibility of even being able to measure the consensus of the masses in the absence of the appropriate instruments of investigation. Systematic polls did not exist in the Fascist regime and the documentation regarding the "public spirit," as it was called, provides oscillating and contrasting views throughout Italy and over different time periods. The second reason regards the difficulty of being able to investigate, even if the appropriate tools were available, the consensus of the population living in a totalitarian regime which negated every possibility of freely expressing its views. Phil expressed his doubts on consensus seven years after the publication of *La fabbrica del consenso* in his book review of Victoria De Grazia's book on the *dopolavoro*, *The Culture of Consent*, published in 1981. Specifically, on the idea of consensus, Phil observed:

> Arguments concerning the nature of the consensus achieved through the *dopolavoro* are not . . . easily resolved. The problem of 'consensus' has in fact been central to the historiographical debate in Fascism ever since the publication of the later volumes of Renzo De Felice's biography of Mussolini. De Grazia appears to agree with De Felice that the regime achieved a considerable degree of consensus, that it reached its apex at the end of the Italo-Ethiopian war, and that it declined rapidly over the next few years. Naturally, De Grazia contends that the *dopolavoro* contributed significantly to that early success, largely because it reinforced values already held by segments of the population that the regime had

---

[21] R. De Felice, *Mussolini il duce. Gli anni del consenso, 1929-1936* (Torino: Einaudi, 1974).

'officially sanctioned' and 'appropriated'. The difficulty, of course, is that in a dictatorship reliable indices of popular attitudes do not exist, so that historians must make deductions and assumptions based on circumstantial, indirect evidence (including cultural content analysis, institutional membership patterns, contemporary commentary, police reports, and official policy statements). De Grazia does just that, and her conclusions must therefore be regarded, like those of other scholars who have tackled this thorny problem, as tentative."[22]

Thus, if, as Cannistraro affirmed, and I completely agree with his assessment, every investigation of consensus is destined to remain "tentative," it follows that this issue should not be considered a barrier to trying to understand the Fascist regime, the organization of the Fascist state, the role and function of the Fascist party, the politics of the masses, the militarization of society, the regimentation of the people, and even the cultural politics and the propaganda apparatus of the "fabbrica del consenso."

From my point of view, all of these apparatus and aspects of the Fascist regime must be analyzed first and foremost as part of the "fabbrica del potere"—the factory of totalitarian power—as instruments through which Mussolini and the party dreamed of reinforcing and expanding their domination, their rule, far more than as a means of trying to attain the consensus of the masses.

This does not negate the importance of the problem of consensus in the Fascist regime, but it does mean we must reexamine it in light of what was new and specific to Fascism as a "fabbrica" of totalitarian power, whose foundations were the police, the militia, the capillary organizations of the party, the prevention and repression of dissent, and the obligatory regimentation of the individual and the masses according to methods, principles, ideals and purposes that did not concede even one iota to the democratic principle that the power of the state depended on the approval of the governed. The term "consensus" has been the cause of endless polemics without any conclusion because it is intrinsically inconclusive, given the impossibility of ascertaining beyond a reasonable doubt what was the actual attachment of the Italians to the Fascist regime, since we do not have a mass of direct information that allows us to assess con-

---

[22] P.V. Cannistraro, "Review of *The Culture of Consent: Mass Organization of Leisure in Fascist Italy* by Victoria De Grazia," *American Historical Review* 87.4 (October 1982), 1129-1130.

sensus. Since 1988 I've expressed my doubts over the ways in which the problem of consensus has been treated and discussed in the historiography of Fascism, agreeing with Cannistraro that on this question every judgment must remain necessarily hypothetical or partial; maybe it was possible for a particular segment of the population, for a particular time period, but it is difficult to assume consensus to be the case for the entire population over the entire time Fascism was in power. As I noted at that time:

> We are facing one of the most complex and controversial problems of Fascism. It is difficult to evaluate, because of the lack of specific analysis as well as because of the fluidity of the phenomenon of consensus, what amounts to 'consent' in a totalitarian regime that is beyond the party card. Any generalization would be misleading. To exclude the presence of 'consent' would be as unrealistic and illusory as to presume a lasting and uniform general adhesion. The analysis of 'consent' should necessarily be divided into different segments, sorted by social condition, place, time, sex, age, and then go on to look at the individualization of the motivations and main sources of this 'consent' (the myth of Mussolini, the image of fascism, the actions of the party, etc.). In the case of the party we have pointed out some of the aspects of 'consent' which, with different levels of intensity, were obtained through a monopoly on political activity and the institutionalization of political professionalism, charity work, entertainment for the masses, and the organization and mobilization of the youth. However, speaking generally about the relationship between the party and the populace, we must point out that at the end of the 1930s there were many symptoms revealing greater negative reactions that were provoked by the policy of the party, the more intrusive and oppressive its obsession with organizing and mobilizing became.[23]

The resources for determining the consent of the population to Fascism are in large part indirect, except for the testimonies derived from letters, diaries and oral histories, which are scarce or limited to only some sections of the population. As to indirect sources, such as the reports on public opinion, either pro or anti-Fascist, contained in archival documents

---

[23] E. Gentile, "Le rôle du parti dans le laboratoire totalitaire italien," translated by Mariangela Portelli, *Annales. Histoire, Sciences Sociales* 43. 3 (May-June 1988), 585-586.

and in the contemporary press, those are certainly more numerous, covering all of Italy over a long arc of time, especially the numerous reports by the prefects, the police, the carabinieri, the PNF, the MVSN, and the OVRA, as well as the reports on the situation in Italy drawn from militant Antifascist sources and conserved in the archives of the Fascist police, and the reports drawn from Communist militants conserved in the archives of the Italian Communist Party. It is to these reports that historians have been generally drawn in order to evaluate the level of consensus Italians had to the Fascist regime. But these sources, as anyone who has studied them in a deep and systematic way knows, and not just occasionally, often lend themselves to paradoxical interpretations: in fact, what occurs for certain periods is that Fascist sources show alarm at the weakness of consensus, or a growing diffusion of dissent to the regime, while Antifascist sources describe a growing adhesion of the masses to the regime.

There is another problem with the "fabbrica del consenso" that deals with the question of totalitarian fascism, maybe the most controversial point, but also the most misunderstood, either because of an ignorance of effective terminology, both historical and conceptual, on the question of totalitarianism, or because of its deliberate deformation. We don't need to consider here those that negate the concept of totalitarian Fascism altogether, either because they believe totalitarianism never existed, or because they believe Fascism was never totalitarian, as were Communism and Nazism. (This last position is shared by the majority of neo-Fascists, who consider Fascism benevolently, as an authoritarian, modernizing and beneficent regime. It is also shared by some neo-Antifascists, who believe the interpretation of Fascism as totalitarian is an "anti-Antifascist" interpretation, but they ignore the fact that the Antifascists themselves derived the concept of totalitarianism and applied it to Fascism.[24]) The most common reason for misunderstanding totalitarian Fascism (though this misunderstanding extends also to Soviet and Nazi totalitarianism) derives from, in part, the confusion of totalitarianism with consensus, and then from the identification of totalitarianism with the *goal* of Fascism (as with the goals of Communism or Nazism). That is to say, on the one hand, the totalitarian regime is understood as a one-party state that man-

[24] See E. Gentile, "Fascism, Totalitarianism and Political Religion: Definitions and Critical Reflections on Criticism of an Interpretation," *Totalitarian Movements and Political Religion* 5.3 (2004), 326-375.

aged to *obtain* the maximum consensus from the maximum number of people; on the other hand, that Fascism, Communism and Nazism only *dreamt* of this goal. The evident paradox of these historiographical interpretations is evident, even though not a few historians have been a victim of this paradox and continue to be.

I believe one can only escape from this paradox by giving back to the concept of totalitarianism its original historical meaning, which would also allow us to revisit the question of consensus in the Fascist regime, getting beyond the long and unfruitful arguments between "consensus yes," "consensus no," "consensus yes and no," to evaluating if the question of consensus is actually critical to the study and interpretation of the Fascist phenomenon—giving back to the concept of totalitarianism its original historical meaning means interpreting totalitarianism as a means and not as a goal, as an instrument to attain a goal and not the goal attained. The Antifascists that coined and elaborated the concept of totalitarianism between 1923 and 1925 were not only referring to the ideology, intentions, ambitions and goals of Fascism, but were also referring to the concrete reality of Fascism as it was from its first months in power. Totalitarian Fascism, as they saw it, was the organization of an armed party that used violence to obtain, conserve, impose and extend the monopoly of state power, establishing a one-party state—"la fabbrica del potere."

The "fabbrica del potere" does not exclude the "fabbrica del consenso," but one must realize that the achievement of consensus was not the primary objective of Fascism while in power, nor a necessary and indispensable condition for its existence. If consensus was the primary objective of Mussolini and Fascism, then after the success of the Ethiopian war and the Munich compromise the regime would have devoted itself principally to the work of conserving the supposed consensus the regime enjoyed with the Italian population, by giving the Italians the peace and stability that they were asking for, demands which were clear from innumerable documents, mostly from Fascist sources, and which accumulated daily on Mussolini's desk. These endless demands for peace infuriated him and caused him to launch invectives against those Italians that thought of nothing but peace and well-being.

It is difficult to consider Fascism as a demagogic regime preoccupied with attracting the consensus of the masses; certainly it did not seek this consensus by giving the masses what they desired, "by courting the masses," as I observed in 1996, "with the promise of material comfort and a peaceful and happy life, by sheltering them from the dangers of war and the convulsions of the modern world at a time when aggressive nationalism and revolutionary ideologies were still dominant."[25] In fact, especially in the late Thirties, we find a regime that declared in an ever more frank and brutal fashion its hatred for peace and its passion for war, that launched continued campaigns against peace and well-being as the ideals of the Fascist life, and that intensified its capillary control and oppression of the population the more the population resisted and became intolerant of the maniacal restrictions of totalitarianism. During the Thirties, the "fabbrica del potere totalitario" intensified its productivity, accelerated the development of the totalitarian state, even to the detriment of the "fabbrica del consenso." And thus, Fascism followed and put into practice, as it had right from the beginning, in its dealings with individuals and the masses, as with its dealings with intellectuals and with culture, a process of integration and regimentation in which the maximum consensus requested was no more than the consensus that military commanders request of their soldiers, whose sole reason for existing was to "believe, obey, and fight."

It was these issues that I discussed with Phil during our last conversations. The echo of his responses are in the books that I have written and published since his passing, thus allowing me to continue my conversations with him—as I have done here today, with you.

---

[25] Gentile, *The Origins of Fascist Ideology*, 368.

FACTORIES AND THEIR PRODUCTS
A COMMENT ON PHILIP CANNISTRARO'S *LA FABBRICA DEL CONSENSO*[1]

Paul Corner

Philip Cannistraro's pioneering study of the fascist attempt to realise a 'cultural revolution' in Italy through the very novel use of the developing mass media provides us with an essential component of a broader picture of the regime. Indeed, it is a mark of the work's originality and quality that this broader picture has been formed largely over the years subsequent to the publication of *La fabbrica del consenso*; studies produced in later years have shown the accuracy of Cannistraro's initial approach to the question and, if these studies have sometimes refined the analysis and added important detail, they have essentially built on that approach and done nothing to alter the initial insights offered by the work. Yet, in one respect, the book is rather surprising. Cannistraro details in very impressive fashion the workings of the propaganda machine; the contributions of cinema, radio and press to the fascist cause are all examined meticulously and the various projects are shown to be very impressive in scope and intention. He makes it clear that the fascist objective of binding the population to the fascist cause through the control of information and the dissemination of propaganda was of primary importance for the regime and represented a central aspect of the relationship between the fascist party and the people. The attempts made to saturate both time and space with fascist symbols and fascist meanings were immense and did constitute a really original aspect of the regime. Cannistraro documents all this with great attention and clear appreciation of the ambition and the novelty of the project (indeed, at times, through his pages, we almost want the innovators to win!). Yet, on several occasions and almost in asides to the main topic, he tells us that the project was a failure—indeed he writes that the *Ministero di Cultura Popolare* (the Orwellian *MinCulPop*) was 'a clamorous failure' (132). Some of the reasons for this failure are given in

---

[1] Philip V. Cannistraro, *La fabbrica del consenso. Fascismo e mass media,* prefazione di Renzo De Felice (Rome-Bari: Laterza, 1975).

the book. There are, for example, those related to the internal workings of the media machine itself (workings which sometimes duplicated themselves, sometimes left gaping holes), to the lack of the resources needed for effective realisation, and to the rivalries between members of the fascist hierarchy who had responsibility for the different sectors of the media and tried to twist them to their own personal and private ends. These are all what might be termed supply-side problems, linked to the questions of organisation, methods of communication, and–sometimes–technology. But the overall issue of the *reception* of the message the media factory was trying to put over–the demand side–is not really tackled. How ordinary people were influenced by the media and what they thought of the various efforts made by the regime to use the media to its advantage are themes which are not covered in the book, except by the broad recognition that the fascist efforts were a failure. Cannistraro acknowledges in his conclusions that the fascist message was not getting over as was intended but does not elaborate on the question; he suggests that it is a problem that goes beyond the scope of the study and that, in any case, it would be very difficult to measure degrees of reception–something which is undoubtedly true.

More recent research, particularly on the 1930s, permits us to put Cannistraro's work into a context which can help to provide an answer to this last question. *La fabbrica del consenso* no longer stands alone; various scholars have charted in different ways the capacity of the regime to extend its influence to most areas of Italian life during the 1930s.[2] The network of institutions and the bureaucratic control exercised by these institutions has been shown to be very extensive and to have been growing all the time, to the degree that we are invited to consider what has sometimes been called, perhaps originally rather loosely, the 'totalitarian' phase of the regime (following the Ethiopian war) in terms of a genuine totalitarianism. In his writings on Adelchi Serena, the head of the fascist party between 1940-41, Emilio Gentile has described an authentically to-

---

[2] See, for example, Philip Morgan, "'The Party is Everywhere': The Italian fascist party in economic life, 1926-40," *English Historical Review*, 114 (1999); Tommaso Baris, *Il fascismo in provincia. Politica e realtà a Frosinone (1919-1940)* (Rome-Bari: Laterza, 2001); Antonello Baù, "Tra prefetti e federali. Note sul Fascismo padovano degli anni trenta," *Storia e problemi contemporanei*, 46 (2007); Loreto Di Nucci, *Lo Stato-partito del fascismo. Genesi, evoluzione e crisi 1919-1943* (Bologna: Il Mulino, 2009); Guido Melis, ed., *Lo Stato negli anni Trenta. Istituzioni e regimi fascisti in Europa* (Bologna: Il Mulino, 2008).

talitarian mind at work (too serious for Mussolini, it seems, who sacked him when he claimed a role for the party too great for the *Duce*'s liking).[3] In fact, it no longer seems possible to doubt that the totalitarian aspirations of fascism were serious and that the regime, in some respects–particularly in terms of regimentation of the population and of social control–went a long way towards the realisation of these aspirations. By the end of the 1930s, fascist saturation of space and time was massive; as Mussolini had hoped, the party was 'everywhere' and almost impossible to avoid.[4] The extensive use of the mass media, which Cannistraro documents so thoroughly, fits into this picture very well.

At the same time, much of the information we have about the *reaction* of large sections of the population to this increased totalitarian thrust suggests that the project did not produce the anticipated results. Renzo De Felice, who famously argued for the existence of widespread consensus for the regime in the period 1929-34[5]–and I think he was right in some ways, although I'm not sure that what was going on can really be described adequately as 'mass consensus'–was one of the first to notice rapidly increasing depoliticisation, apathy, and disgust with politics among the mass of Italians in the later 1930s.[6] This squares with my own, more recent, research on the workings of the provincial fascist federations in the later 1930s–research which has served to confirm this movement of opinion away from the regime. For a variety of reasons, those attitudes which are grouped together for the early 1930s under the term of 'consensus'–these include, certainly, compliance, collaboration, an inevitable complicity, all more or less enforced at popular level by the repressive context of the regime, but also undoubtedly some degree of appreciation of what the regime was doing, or said it would do, in many areas–are replaced by attitudes which reflect a greater hostility to the regime and a growing cynicism about what "real existing fascism" represented. By late 1938 and for all of 1939 police and party informers were reporting that a previous ambiguity of opinion had disappeared in many quarters, that

---

[3] Emilio Gentile, *La via italiana al totalitarismo: il partito e lo Stato nel regime fascista* (Rome: NIS, 1995).

[4] Mussolini's sentiment expressed in a speech of 1929, quoted in Alberto Aquarone, *L'organizzazione dello stato totalitario* (Turin: Einaudi, 1965).

[5] Renzo De Felice, *Mussolini il duce: gli anni del consenso, 1929-1936* (Turin: Einaudi, 1974).

[6] Documented in my chapter in Paul Corner, ed., *Popular Opinion in Totalitarian Regimes. Fascism, Nazism, Communism* (Oxford: Oxford University Press, 2009). Translated as *Il consenso totalitario* (Rome-Bari: Laterza, 2012).

hostility was being voiced openly, and no longer privately, 'by all classes' and that rumours of popular revolt were on everyone's lips.[7] Much of this antagonism was determined by the behaviour of provincial fascist leaders, who often used their power for personal and private ends–making money, favouring their families and relations, effecting personal vendettas and exacting favours.[8] It was an antagonism generated not only by corruption and malpractice of what people called '*la casta*' but also and increasingly by the very obvious and ever-widening gap between fascist promises and their realisation. After nearly twenty years the glorious fascist future seemed ever further away (empire did little to reassure people, it seems) and there is no evidence of the creation of that 'dual reality' which kept the Soviet Union afloat in certain periods, encouraging people to accept appalling conditions of life and work in the present because they were convinced they were building a better socialist future. In Italy, by the late 1930s, the fascist future looked extremely bleak, thanks to what was widely perceived to be a foolish alliance with Hitler, which brought with it the prospect of a major European war. What informers reported consistently was that the distance between the local representatives of the regime and popular sentiment had grown enormously, with ordinary people unable to stand any longer the requirements of the party and the pretensions of its second-rank leaders. In their reports prefects also spoke frequently about public apathy for the regime and commented on public dislike of and disdain for the 'little Mussolini's' of the provinces.

Thus we can begin to see a dual process taking place in the later 1930s. On the one hand, at an institutional level, the regime was tightening its grip on the population. This was true in terms of repression–people began to complain that 'there are ears listening everywhere' and warned each other that a remark overheard by a spy could provoke ruin– and also because, in important developments, the *Partito Nazionale Fascista* managed to reinforce its position in respect of the state institutions (which, translated to the provincial level, meant the *federale* having more authority in respect of the prefect). On the other hand–and partly as a result of this tightening grip–any popular consensus for the regime declined dramatically, even before the entry in war in 1940. There is thus an

---

[7] See Paul Corner, *The Fascist Italy and Popular Opinion in Mussolini's Italy* (Oxford: Oxford University Press, 2012), chapter 9.
[8] Ibid., chapter 8.

increasing split between regime activity–very high–and popular respect for the regime–declining sharply.

Read in this context of increasing division, *La fabbrica del consenso* finds its place perfectly. In showing the enormous efforts which went into the attempt to form a fascist culture and to disseminate that culture to the masses, the study confirms the totalitarian pretensions of the regime. But equally, in speaking of the failure of the project, the book also confirms the problems the regime faced in convincing the population of its message. Cannistraro's study can be related very profitably to both sides of the equation, therefore–to the intentions of the regime (the project) and to the realisations in terms of popular acceptance of these intentions. To some extent the study can be compared to another, almost contemporaneous, work–that of Victoria De Grazia on the *Opera Nazionale Dopolavoro*–and to her conclusions, couched in terms of the contrast between the very high levels of organisation of the *Dopolavoro* and the low degree of acceptance of the political message proclaimed by its leaders.[9] And, in this second respect (reception), we are now better placed to answer the question which remained unanswered in Cannistraro's study–that of the reasons for the refusal of the population to accept the message of the fascist media in such a way as to participate fully in a fascist popular culture. Put very simply, it seems that the propaganda was not saying what people wanted to hear. Cannistraro notes that the radio repeated the same slogans for years on end; people became bored and then irritated by them. Police informers protested repeatedly to their bosses about the quality of fascist propaganda; the continuous heralding of the achievements of the regime contrasted too obviously with what people saw around them and informers reported that such propaganda was counter-productive–it offended rather than reassured. Newspapers fawned persistently on fascist 'realisations', but ordinary people said, when they bought the paper, 'give me six lira of lies'. One fascist informer explained, in early 1939, why people looked for foreign newspapers if they could find them: 'here–he wrote–there isn't even a dog who has had any credibility among the population for years'. Others made the same remarks about the fact that, in 1938, many people were tuning in to Radio Barcelona rather than listening to fascist radio in order to find out what was

---

[9] Victoria De Grazia, *The Culture of Consent: Mass Organisation of Leisure in Fascist Italy* (Cambridge: Cambridge University Press, 1981).

going on. The informers were irritated by the fact that what came from abroad was considered to be true, what came from the authorities in Rome considered automatically to be false. From what we know, this was very far from being the case in Nazi Germany.

So, in conclusion, it seems that, over the years and despite the best efforts of *MinCulPop*, the fascist message became increasingly difficult to believe. The message itself was demonstrably false, unpalatable and hard to stomach; so, very often, were the messengers (and, in a regime which had claimed initially to legitimate itself through a clean-up of political practice, this last point should not be underestimated: after all, most people judged fascism through their contacts with local fascists). The message was there, proclaimed through press, radio and cinema and daubed on the sides of thousands of houses throughout Italy. But it failed to convince. What Philip Cannistraro's *La fabbrica del consenso* shows us so well is that horses can be brought to the water by all manner of devices; the problem is making them drink—and this may depend, in turn, on the quality of the water. In a way, this is a reassuring conclusion. Less reassuring, for the present, is the consideration that, while the quality of the political water may not always have improved all that much since fascist times (Berlusconi *docet*), methods of making us drink–the new factories of consensus–have certainly become very much more refined.

MARINETTI AND THE CULT OF THE DUCE

Ernest Ialongo

Filippo Tommaso Marinetti has the unlikely distinction of being quite famous, but in many ways quite unknown. To many, he was the leader of the Italian Futurist art movement that exploded onto the modern art world in Milan in 1909, and lasted all the way until Marinetti's death in December of 1944. Marinetti the Futurist was best known for his embrace of modern technology and a modern culture that glorified speed, power, action, and above all, the dominance over the natural world that such modern technology promised. One cannot talk of the representation of the airplane, the automobile, the dreadnought battleship, modern industry and the city in modern culture without encountering Futurism.[1]

Marinetti's goal was to modernize Italy, to drag it out of the cultural backwater and tourist trap it had become since its glory days in the Renaissance. And to accomplish this, one had to destroy all that was old, traditional, and an obstacle to the youthful energies that would shape modern Italy. Thus, in the Foundation Manifesto we read Marinetti's declaration that the Futurists "wish to destroy museums, libraries, [and] academies of any sort," but will glorify "the pulsating, nightly ardor of arsenals and shipyards, . . . railway stations, voraciously devouring smoke-belching serpents, . . . [and] the lissome flight of the airplane, whose propeller flutters like a flag in the wind, seeming to applaud, like a crowd excited."[2] In a subsequent declaration we read of Marinetti's desire to "triumph" over both the Vatican and the Monarchy—two further bastions of the conservative order.[3]

---

[1] Robert Wohl covers the Futurists and the airplane in his *A Passion for Wings: Aviation and the Western Imagination, 1908-1918* (New Haven, CT: Yale University Press, 1994). Marinetti specifically refers to the automobile in the "Foundation and Manifesto of Futurism" (1909), and the dreadnought in the "Second Political Manifesto" (1911). For these documents see F.T. Marinetti, *Critical Writings*, edited by Günter Berghaus, translated by Doug Thompson (New York: Farrar, Strauss and Giroux, 2006), 12, 74.

[2] Marinetti *Critical Writings,* 14.

[3] Marinetti, "Third Futurist Political Manifesto," (1913), in Marinetti, *Critical Writings*, 76.

Of course, the other fact that many people know about Marinetti, and which did not get much prominence in the 2009 centenary celebrations of Futurism's foundation, was that Marinetti was a pronounced nationalist, and, consequently, as Benito Mussolini called him, a "fervent" Fascist.[4] Marinetti first met Mussolini during the interventionist crisis of 1915, when they both helped force Italy into World War One. Marinetti was at the founding meeting of the Italian Fascist Party in 1919. He fought alongside the Fascists against the Socialists throughout 1919. And he ran on the Fascist ticket in the November 1919 elections. And, although he bolted from the party in 1920—owing to what he called its increasingly reactionary nature—after 1922, when Mussolini became Prime Minister, Marinetti was an energetic and consistent propagandist for the emerging Duce.[5]

This brings me to the subject of my paper. I believe that one of the most important roles that Marinetti performed for Mussolini was to help shape his image, and the image of the Fascist state, as quintessentially modern. Throughout the years of Mussolini's reign, 1922-1945, there was a constant struggle to define and shape the Duce, and by extension Fascism, in an attempt to influence which policies the state would follow. From the beginning, Marinetti was committed to shaping the developing cult of the Duce as the embodiment of modern, Futurist principles—

---

[4] Yvon De Begnac, *Taccuini mussoliniani*, edited by Francesco Perfetti (Bologna: Il Mulino, 1990), 307.

[5] There are a number of works dealing with political Futurism, but they generally focus on the early years of Futurism (1909-1920), and none provide a thorough treatment of Marinetti's contributions to the Fascist regime. See: Günter Berghaus, *Futurism and Politics: Between Anarchist Rebellion and Fascist Reaction, 1909-1944* (Providence, RI: Berghahn Books, 1996); Enrico Crispolti, *Storia e critica del futurismo*, 2nd ed. (Rome: Editori Laterza, 1987); Emilio Gentile, "Il futurismo e la politica. Dal nazionalismo modernista al fascismo (1909-1920)," in *Futurismo, Cultura, e Politica*, edited by Renzo de Felice (Turin: Fondazione Giovanni Agnelli, 1988); Giovanni Lista, *Arte e politica: Il futurismo di sinistra in Italia* (Milan: Multhipla, 1980); Gian Battista Nazzaro, *Futurismo e politica* (Naples: J.N. Editore S.p.A., 1987); Claudia Salaris, *Marinetti: Arte e vita futurista* (Rome: Riuniti, 1997); *Storia del futurismo: Libri, giornali, manifesti* (Rome: Riuniti, 1992); Salaris, *Artecrazia: L'avanguardia futurista negli anni del fascismo* (Scandicci: Nuova Italia, 1992); Marja Härmänmaa, *Un patriota che sfidò la decadenza. F.T. Marinetti e l'idea dell'uomo nuovo fascista, 1929-1940* (Helsinki: Academia Scientiarum Fennica, 2000); Enzo Santarelli, "Il movimento politico futurista," in *Fascismo e neofascismo: studi e problemi di ricerca*, edited by Enzo Santarelli (Rome: Editori Riuniti, 1974); Umberto Carpi, "Sovversivismo anti borghese e borghesia sovversiva: appunti sull'ideologia del 'primo futurismo'," *Lavoro Critico* 25 (January/April, 1982): 5-38.

revolutionary in all things, challenging the old order, and above all, the promoter of a modern, Italian culture.[6]

Certainly, this was an initiative that was beneficial to both Marinetti and Mussolini. To Marinetti, if he could successfully portray the Duce as modern, it would leave far more room for maneuver for his modern art movement within the regime, especially as he weathered attacks from conservative and anti-modernist Fascists who similarly sought to shape the regime's policies. For Mussolini, having Marinetti as such a fervent ally, associating Futurism with Fascism, allowed him to combat the image propagated by anti-Fascists: that Fascism was a movement devoid of any cultural or ideological depth, a reactionary movement that was committed simply to saving capitalism—its revolutionary rhetoric notwithstanding—and a movement that had no real support and remained in power purely through repressive means.[7]

It is not my intention to argue the validity or invalidity of Renzo De Felice's contention that in the years 1929 to 1936 the Duce enjoyed, on a certain level, the consensus or popular support of the Italian people.[8] The recent work by Paul Corner, Mauro Canali and Mimmo Franzinelli on the efficacy of the Italian dictatorship at limiting dissent through its secret and political police forces, as well as by simply limiting access to state services, have shown the difficulty in trying to measure genuine support for the regime.[9] Instead, I would like to focus on the battle to shape the cult of the Duce within Italy, and to suggest that Marinetti's initiatives may have had some effect if we look at some of the policies inaugurated

---

[6] All biographies of Mussolini narrate this political balancing act. Some of the most recent which are good on this include Martin Clark, *Mussolini* (London: Longman, 2005) and Richard Bosworth, *Mussolini* (London: Arnold Publishers, 2002). The classic in this area still remains Adrian Lyttelton, *The Seizure of Power: Fascism in Italy, 1919-1929,* 2nd edition (London: Weidenfeld and Nicolson, 1987; 1st edition, 1973).

[7] For a general overview of the anti-Fascist view, see Renzo De Felice, *Fascism: An Informal Introduction to its Theory and Practice,* edited by Michael Ledeen (New Brunswick, NJ: Transaction Books, 1976; originally published as *Intervista sul fascismo* [Bari: Laterza, 1975]).

[8] Renzo De Felice, *Mussolini: Il duce,* part 1, *Gli anni del consenso, 1929-1936* (Turin: Einaudi, 1974).

[9] Paul Corner, "Italian Fascism: What Ever Happened to Dictatorship?," *The Journal of Modern History* 74 (June 2002): 325-351; Mimmo Franzinelli, *I tentacoli dell'Ovra: agenti, collaboratori e vittime della polizia politica fascista* (Turin: Bollati Boringhieri, 1999); Mauro Canali, *Le spie del regime* (Bologna: Il Mulino, 2004). See also the essays by Emilio Gentile and Paul Corner in this volume.

by the regime, as well as the overwhelming resistance Marinetti met with both within Italy and internationally.

The first step in Marinetti's drive to shape the image of the Duce and the regime was the presentation of his *Diritti artistici propugnati dai futuristi italiani* (the *Artistic Rights Proposed by Italian Futurists*) to Mussolini just weeks after he took office. The *Diritti artistici* sought to transform the Italian state into an active promoter and patron of modern Italian art.[10] Under the Liberal government, Marinetti had declared that one of the Futurist's goals was to end the "meddling of government in matters of art."[11] However, with Mussolini, Marinetti felt he could harness the Fascist government in the interests of modern Italian art, as both men were committed to mobilizing culture in the interests of national unity and strength.[12] The *Diritti artistici*, for instance, requested that the state mandate the presence of Italian artists, and specifically modern Italian artists, in all exhibitions in Italy which were supported by the national or by local governments, such as the Venice Biennale, which had been roundly attacked for admitting French and Russian modern artists, but not Italian ones.[13] To further develop the modern arts, the *Diritti artistici* called for the abolition of all academies, institutes of art and professional schools to be replaced by free, state-funded schools that would train instructors to teach modern art techniques. The state was also to fund free art competitions throughout the nation, so that new artists could be discovered without being stifled by the artistic bureaucracy. Marinetti further requested institutes of artistic propaganda, which would promote Italian art overseas. Finally, the *Diritti artistici* called for the state to subsidize artists while

---

[10] The draft can be found in Archivio Centrale dello Stato [ACS], Presidenza del Consiglio dei Ministri, 1923, B. 710, f. 3.11.313. An English translation has recently become available in F.T. Marinetti, *Critical Writings*, 357-363.

[11] Marinetti, "Third Political Manifesto," 76.

[12] Marinetti recounts a war-time conversation with Mussolini in which they both lamented the artists and intellectuals who refused to engage in the conflict. See the entry dated July 20, 1918, in F.T. Marinetti, *Taccuini, 1915-1921*, edited by Alberto Bertoni (Bologna: Il Mulino, 1987), 287.

[13] "Diritti artistici propugnati dai Futuristi italiani," ACS. For Marinetti's view on the Biennale's policy, see F.T. Marinetti, "Vittorio Pica è un idiota," in *Roma futurista*, March 14, 1920. This article was an endorsement of the original protest launched by Margherita Sarfatti against Pica in her "L'avanguardia artistica italiana e gli inviti alle Biennali di Venezia," in *Il Popolo d'Italia*, February 29, 1920. Also see Philip V. Cannistraro and Brian R. Sullivan, *Il Duce's Other Woman* (New York: William Morrow and Company, Inc., 1993), 223.

they produced their work, and to help allay the costs of mounting an exhibition.[14]

Marinetti justified this close relationship between the state and modern culture in Italy by arguing that, just as Futurism was a revolutionary art movement, Fascism was a revolutionary political movement—which had its roots in political Futurism—and the two must work together for the advancement of modern Italy. This was the point Marinetti made explicit in a second version of the *Diritti artistici* which he circulated amongst a number of Futurists for their commentary, and which was ultimately published in the Fascist newspaper *L'Impero* in March 1923.[15] In it he argued that "the advent of Fascism to power constitute[s] the realization of the minimum Futurist program, launched (with a maximum program not yet fulfilled) 14 years ago by a group of audacious youth that put themselves in opposition to [an] entire Nation poisoned by senility. . . . [16]

Marinetti continued shaping the image of the Duce in ever more public fashion through the rest of the 1920s. In March 1924 he published the book *Futurismo e Fascismo* whose goal was to present Fascism as the logical political evolution of the revolutionary principles Futurism had been propagating since 1909.[17] In the preface to the book Marinetti made clear that "this book presents to the reader Futurism and Fascism, the influence of the first on the second, the political alliance of the two movements and the differences that distinguish them."[18] In referring to the Futurist influence on Fascism, Marinetti was specifically associating Fascism with the

---

[14] "Diritti artistici propugnati dai Futuristi italiani," ACS.

[15] F.T. Marinetti et al., "I Diritti artistici propugnati dai futuristi italiani, Manifesto al Governo fascista," in F.T. Marinetti, *Teoria e invenzione futurista* [*TIF*], edited by Luciano De Maria (Verona: Mondadori, 1968), 489-495. The manifesto was published in the inaugural issue of *L'Impero* on March 11, 1923. See De Maria, "Nota ai testi," in F.T. Marinetti, *TIF*, CXIII; F.T. Marinetti, *Critical Writings*, 363.

[16] F.T Marinetti et al., "I Diritti artistici propugnati dai futuristi italiani, Manifesto al Governo fascista," in *Fillia e l'avanguardia futurista negli anni del fascismo*, edited by Silvia Evangelisti (Milan: Arnoldo Mondadori, 1986), 308. The original is located in the Filippo Tommaso Marinetti Papers, Beinecke Rare Book and Manuscript Library, Yale University [YMP], Box 23, Folder 1274 and Box 54, Folder 2001. The marginalia appears in the version located in Box 54, Folder 2001. Analyses of the draft are also available in Berghaus, *Futurism and Politics*, 193-196 and Nazzaro, *Futurismo e politica*, 166-167.

[17] F.T. Marinetti, *Futurismo e Fascismo* (Foligno: Franco Campitelli, 1924); reprinted in F.T. Marinetti, *TIF*.

[18] F.T. Marinetti, "Prefazione," in Marinetti, *TIF*, 432.

Futurist goal of eradicating all traditionalist obstacles that hindered Italy's emergence as a modern nation. Just as importantly, Marinetti's claim that there were differences between Futurism and Fascism was a direct assault on the conservative and anti-modernist elements within Fascism. The entire book laid out a narrative of Futurism and Fascism that made the incontrovertible claim that the latter was intimately rooted in the former. In a series of short chapters Marinetti narrated his relationship with Mussolini that began in 1915 and went right up to the founding of the Fascist Party and beyond, essentially making the claim that even before there was a Fascism, Mussolini was sympathetic to Futurism.[19] The book, incidentally, was dedicated "Al mio caro e grande amico Benito Mussolini."

The next venue wherein Marinetti would continue his public shaping of the Duce's image occurred at the Convention of Fascist Intellectuals held in March 1925, when the stakes over the image of Fascism were higher than anything to date. Through the latter half of 1924 Mussolini faced the Matteotti Crisis after the Socialist deputy Giacomo Matteotti had been murdered by Fascists close to Mussolini. Matteotti had disappeared after he protested the fraudulent nature of the 1924 parliamentary elections which had given the Fascists control of the legislature. When his body turned up, Mussolini's government was threatened on multiple fronts. On the one hand, he faced the boycott of parliament by Socialists and Liberals who refused to recognize the legitimacy of the Fascist government once its connection to Matteotti's murder was clear. On the other, Mussolini faced the hostility of Fascist intransigents which insisted he eliminate democracy once and for all and crush Fascism's opponents. Consequently, in January 1925 Mussolini imposed the dictatorship, eliminating freedom of the press, assembly, and representative government.[20] However, with the imposition of the dictatorship, the anti-Fascists, at home and abroad, were provided with all the fodder they needed to define Fascism as nothing more than organized thuggery. To wit, Mussolini called for the Convention of Fascist Intellectuals, which, he declared, would "end once and for all the foolish myth of an incompatibility be-

---

[19] See, for instance "I futuristi nella lotta fascista," " 'Il Popolo d'Italia,' 'Roma Futurista' e fondazione dei Fasci di Combattimento," "La Battaglia di Via Mercanti il 15 aprile 1919 prima vittoria del Fascismo," in F.T. Marinetti, *TIF*, 440-442, 442-448, 448-452, respectively.
[20] For the Matteotti Crisis, see Lyttelton, *The Seizure of Power*, Chapter 10, "The Matteotti Crisis," *passim*; Clark, *Mussolini*, 79-88; Bosworth, *Mussolini*, 194-207.

tween intelligence and Fascism."[21] Or, as the regime newspaper put it, the "convention will demonstrate the consensus of the best members of the Italian intelligentsia for that movement [Fascism] that has been represented as devoid of any intellectual quality, a product of the *manganello* and not of thought."[22]

The very calling of the Convention signaled that Mussolini was going to actively mobilize the intelligentsia in a union of state and culture which Marinetti had been calling for since the beginning of Mussolini's reign. However, just what shape Fascist culture would take was still to be determined, and this was the subject the Convention would deal with. As such, Marinetti attended the Convention and advocated strongly that Fascism was and always would be a modern and revolutionary movement. This was clear, he argued, because of the close relations of Futurism and Fascism since the latter's infancy, a connection that was even recognized by Benedetto Croce, who famously, and publicly, denounced the Convention.[23] Marinetti went so far as to emphasize Mussolini's own Futurist nature through a recitation of a number of passages by the Duce in which he had called for a government of "speed," and a government that would look beyond the glories of the ancient Roman Empire.[24] More importantly, Marinetti argued that modern Italian art was an effective means of building international recognition, and admiration, for Fascist Italy. Just as Gabrielle D'Annunzio had garnered respect for modern Italy by the international fame he had achieved, modern Italian art, and specifically the Futurists, would do the same for Fascist Italy. As such, he called for a state policy to advance the modern arts in line with the *Diritti artistici* first laid before Mussolini in 1922.[25]

Just how successful were Marinetti's efforts at shaping the image of the Duce and the policies of the regime? Certainly we can point to clear connections between Marinettian ideas and Mussolini's cultural policy. To be sure, an official Fascist art was never created. Mussolini derived far more advantage at having modernists like Marinetti compete for his favor

---

[21] Quoted in Emilio Papa, *Storia di due manifesti: Il fascismo e la cultura italiana* (Milan: Feltrinelli, 1958), 50.

[22] "La coltura [sic] nazionale al Convegno fascista di Bologna," in *Il Popolo d'Italia*, March 28, 1925.

[23] F.T. Marinetti, "La camera degli artisti," in Fillia et al, *Arte Fascista: Elementi per la battaglia artistica* (Turin: Sindacati artistici, 1927), 28.

[24] Ibid., 29-30.

[25] Ibid., 28, 30-34.

along with anti-modernists and conservatives. However, the infrastructure of culture was brought under state-control, and thus the basic premises of Marinetti's *Diritti artistici*, wherein the state protects and supports the expansion of modern Italian art, could be realized. For instance, after 1926 all artists were required to be members of their respective syndicates within Mussolini's new corporative state, which sought to rationalize the economy by bringing together all its players into more planned and efficient relationships. Thus, members of the *Sindacato fascista delle belle arti* (Fascist Syndicate of Fine Arts) not only included writers, architects, painters, sculptors and musicians, but also the culture industry itself, and members of the government. All would supposedly work together to support the arts through a combination of subsidies, price regulations, and guaranteed access to exhibitions. Though this system did not solely benefit the modern arts, after the state took over the Venice Biennale of modern art, the Milan Triennale of modern decorative arts, and created the Rome Quadriennale of Italian art, modern Italian artists, specifically the Futurists, had far less trouble finding exhibition space, patrons for their art, or financial help for their craft.[26] Of course, the trade-off for this greater support from the state was a significant loss of artistic autonomy. To exhibit in a show one had to be a member of a syndicate, which required Fascist Party membership in good standing. Thus, economic need often forced artists into apolitical subjects matters, or, on the other extreme, gross opportunism.[27]

The other clear proof of Marinetti's success was the *Mostra della Rivoluzione fascista* (Exhibit of the Fascist Revolution) of 1932, which celebrated the tenth anniversary of the Fascist regime. The exhibit was a visual history of Fascism from 1914 to 1932, and ushered the visitor through a series of rooms that portrayed the chaos and weakness of the pre-Fascist years, followed by the "Fascist Revolution" that had brought Italy national order and strength, as well as international respect. And to depict just how revolutionary and modern Fascism was, Mussolini reached out to a

---

[26] Cannistraro, *La fabbrica del consenso: Fascismo e mass media* (Bari: Laterza, 1975), 32-35; Marla Stone, *The Patron State: Culture and Politics in Fascist Italy* (Princeton, NJ: Princeton University Press, 1998), 25-28. A fine recent survey of the success of the Futurists at the Quadriennale is Gino Agnese et al., *I futuristi e le Quadriennali* (Milan: Electa, 2008).

[27] Cannistraro, *La fabbrica del consenso*, 34-35; Stone, *The Patron State*, 26-28. Stone and Cannistraro disagree over whether one had to be a member of the Fascist Party in order to be a member of a syndicate. Moreover, Stone notes that there were some occasions in which artists could display without membership in a syndicate, though these were not common.

variety of modern art movements, including Futurism, the Novecento, the Rationalists, and the Strapaese, and requested they "produce something contemporary, and thus modern and audacious, without the sad reminders of the decorative styles of the past."[28] Marinetti was somewhat disappointed at the rather limited showing the Futurists had at the exhibit, with most of the important halls given to the Novecentista Mario Sironi.[29] However, he could not have been disappointed that the story of Fascism that was told was as he wanted it—with Mussolini and Fascism depicted as modern and revolutionary. He claimed in his journal *Futurismo* that "the Exhibition of the Fascist Revolution Signals the Triumph of Futurist Art."[30] Though an overstatement, when one considers that many Novecentisti, Rationalists and Strapaesani were once Futurists, and that these were the dominant movements at the *Mostra*, then Marinetti's claim of the Futurist influence on Fascism does not seem so far-fetched.

Perhaps an even more important barometer of Marinetti's success at shaping the image of the Duce as modern and revolutionary was the sheer opposition he encountered at every step of the way. The earliest resistance Marinetti faced came from within the Futurist movement itself. When he distributed a copy of the *Diritti artistici* to the Futurists in early 1923 for their comment, the left-wing Futurists Carlo Frassinelli and Franco Rampa Rossi of Turin were scathing in their commentary. In the preamble to the *Diritti artistici* in which Marinetti argued that Futurism and Fascism were parallel movements that had brought the revolution in art and politics that was modernizing Italy, Frassinelli and Rampa Rossi disagreed with every point. After a section in which Marinetti sought to highlight the Futurists' and Mussolini's joint interventionist activities in 1915, and their joint founding of Fascism in 1919, Rampa Rossi reminded Marinetti that he had in fact left Fascism in 1920 because of its growing reactionary nature. When Marinetti sought to paint Mussolini as a Futurist, declaring that the latter had once told journalists that "We are a young people that wants to and must create, and refuses to be a syndicate of ho-

---

[28] Quoted in *Mostra della Rivoluzione fascista* [catalogue], edited by Dino Alfieri and Luigi Freddi (Rome: Partito nazionale fascista, 1933; reprint edition, Milan: IGIS spa Industrie Grafiche Italiane, 1982), 8.

[29] Specifically the rooms that covered the March on Rome, the Advent of the Fascist Revolution, the Salon of Honor (a glorification of Mussolini), and the Gallery of Fasces (commemorating each of the ten Fascist years in power).

[30] "La Mostra della Rivoluzione Fascista segna il Trionfo dell'Arte Futurista," in *Futurismo*, October 23, 1932.

teliers and museum guardians," Rampa Rossi pointed out that Mussolini had then demanded that he wanted obligatory religious education, exaltation of the monarchy, suppression of workers' organizations and chambers of labor, and the suppression of the free press. Additionally, Rampa Rossi pointed out that "we've seen what the Fascists are good for: to be police, no more no less. Mussolini himself has understood that, and has made them into a police force. We Futurists have always combated *carabinierismo* [a policeman's mentality]. [And] Fascism has created a policeman's mentality." Finally, when Marinetti argued that "With Mussolini Fascism has rejuvenated Italy. We wait for Him to help us in the renewal of the artistic environment, where inauspicious [*nefaste*] men and things [still] remain. The political revolution must sustain the artistic revolution—that is, Futurism and all the avant-gardes," Rampa Rossi responded "Let's stop calling the coming of Fascism a revolution. It has revolutionized none of the old institutions!," and Frassinelli pointed out that "Fascism learned much from the socialist experiences, and thus was not original in its revolutionary aspects, if it wants to call itself that."[31]

In depicting Mussolini as modern and revolutionary, Marinetti faced even more virulent criticism outside his movement on the political right. From 1925 to 1926, *Critica facista*, the regime's cultural journal, ran a series of articles that sought to determine what Fascist art should and should not be. In these articles, modern art, and Futurism specifically, came in for direct attacks. Ardengo Soffici, for instance, with the Futurists in mind, argued that Fascist art could not be something that simply renounced the past completely, "discarding all principles in a revolutionary overturning of all recognizable values. . . ." This Futurist tendency, he argued "has been followed and glorified, logically enough, by Russian Bolshevism," which had adopted Futurism.[32] He criticized the Fascist state as being too soft in its policing of culture, tolerating an art "whose mentality, aesthetics, and forms of artistic expression were in essence and in derivation not only foreign, but more precisely, barbarian, anti-Italian, liberal, Judaic, Masonic, democratic—in a word, antifascist *par excellence*."[33] A few months later, in the journal *L'Arte fascista*, that was similarly debating

---

[31] Ibid., 308-309.
[32] "Ardengo Soffici," in Jeffrey Schnapp and Barbara Spackman, eds., "Selections from the Great Debate on Fascism and Culture: *Critica Fascista* 1926-1927," *Stanford Italian Review*, 8.1-2, "Fascism and Culture," (1990), 240. Appeared in *Critica Fascista* on October 15, 1926.
[33] Ibid., 228.

what Fascist art should be, Marinetti was publicly told by Gesulado Manzella-Frontini that the notion that "today's Italy could export to the world Marinettian and Futurist art . . . as a genuine product of Italianità, with a Fascist label, meaning an art born from the ethico-politico-religious conception of Fascism, is a HERESY, A CONTRADICTION, AND AN AWFUL IDEA."[34] Fascism, he argued, should have an art that aspired to equilibrium and tradition, just as its political and social policies sought.[35] A decade later, as Fascist Italy and Nazi Germany became close allies, Marinetti's claims came under even more vicious attack. Telesio Interlandi, for instance, in 1938 openly condemned Marinetti for his defense of modern art and his association of Futurism with Fascism. He then asked rhetorically,

> must Italy still submit to this inadmissible violence that deters it from its artistic vocation and imposes on it a barbaric aesthetic, born in the gutter of the International and consecrated in the capitals of Jewish and mixed-race cosmopolitism . . . ? Dear Marinetti, you can call us defeatists if you like, you cannot call us imbeciles . . . ; we say no, we reject the "modern" as the biggest fraud that has been perpetuated to the harm of a provincial Italy that today no longer exists. . . . Modern art is a tumor that must be cut, it must not be exhibited as a national glory simply because it is to Marinetti's liking.[36]

The resistance to Marinetti was not simply limited to within Italy. Marinetti traveled throughout Europe, North Africa, and South America trumpeting the glories of the Futurist art movement and the glories of Fascism in Italy, and never ceased making the connection between the two movements. Often he would claim that in Mussolini's totalitarian dictatorship the Duce's appreciation for the modern arts allowed for far greater cultural openness than anti-Fascists cared to admit. This was exactly the line he took with Maurice Bedel, the French novelist and essay-

---

[34] G. Manzella-Frontini, "Romanesimo," in *L'Arte fascista*, 2, 1927, quoted in Claudia Salaris, *Artecrazia: L'avanguardia futurista negli anni del fascismo* (Scandicci: Nuova Italia, 1992), 81. Salaris does not provide a more detailed citation for the journal.

[35] G. Manzella-Frontini, "L'arte facista non sarà l'arte futurista," in *L'Arte fascista*, 9, 1926, quoted in Salaris, *Artecrazia*, 80.

[36] Telesio Interlandi, "Il Dadà di Marinetti," in *Il Tevere*, November 24-25, 1938, excerpted in Enrico Crispolti, *Il mito della macchina e altri temi del futurismo* (Trapani: Celebes, 1969), 740-745. The quote appears on p. 743.

ist, who publicly asked Marinetti in 1929 how he could possibly be so closely associated with the dictator Mussolini.[37] Marinetti's response was simple: Fascism and culture were not incompatible. Benedetto Croce, he argued, in spite of being an anti-Fascist, was still free to publish in Italy, and he, Marinetti, in spite of his rabid anti-clerical sentiments, was not only free to publish his modernist works, even after the Lateran Accords had been signed between the Vatican and the Fascist state, but had been elevated to the Royal Academy of Italy.[38]

However, this explanation was wearing thin by 1929, and was believed by few, if any, people by 1936, when the Fascist dictatorship had been fully developed at home, crushing all real dissent, and Mussolini was now engaged in imperial conquest in Ethiopia. That September, Marinetti led the Italian delegation to the International PEN Congress in Buenos Aires. PEN was committed to freedom of artistic expression everywhere, and consequently became increasingly opposed to the German and Italian dictatorships as the Thirties progressed. At the Argentine PEN Congress Marinetti met with a torrent of abuse for his affiliation with and defense of the Italian dictatorship, especially by the French delegation who had witnessed the surge of fascism in their own country with the fascist riots of February 1934, which had led to the formation of the anti-Fascist Popular Front government of Leon Blum.[39] Marinetti was subsequently drummed out of the PEN Congress.[40] Such was his humiliation, that when France was defeated in 1940 Marinetti spitefully penned a pub-

---

[37] Bedel's letter appeared in *Les Nouvelles Litteraires et Artistiques* of Paris. The date cannot be ascertained, but it likely appeared in mid to late November 1929, as Marinetti's response refers to his conferences on the *Novecento*, which were held on October 18 and mid-November, as happening just a few days before. Moreover, Marinetti held a public conference on his response to Bedel on December 2, 1929. Bedel was not the only Frenchman that publicly commented on Marinetti's nomination. The conservative Camille Mauclaire joked of the "old anarchist and internationalist that became a fiery fascist," in the January 23, 1930 edition of *L'éclaireur de Nice*, quoted in Michel Ostenc, *Intellectuels italiens et fascisme (1915-1929)* (Paris: Payot, 1983), 259.

[38] The article was ultimately published as "Replica a Maurice Bedel," in *Gazzetta del Popolo*, November 29, 1929. However, the analysis above is taken from the Italian draft of this article found in Marinetti's papers at Yale. See, F.T. Marinetti, "Risposta a Maurice Bedel," in YMP, Box 34, Folder 1575: Risposta a Maurice Bedel.

[39] See Eugen Weber's, "A Famous Victory," in his *The Hollow Years: France in the 1930s* (New York: W.W. Norton and Co., 1994), 147-181.

[40] Salaris, *Artecrazia*, 187.

lic letter boasting that Fascism had clearly shown itself to be the superior ideology to French democracy.[41]

Of course this victory was fleeting. In the ensuring years Fascist Italy and Nazi Germany would be stripped of their territorial gains. Mussolini would be toppled in 1943, and reduced to the puppet dictator of the Republic of Salò, eventually to be hunted down and executed by partisans in April 1945. Marinetti followed Mussolini to the north, where he eventually died of a heart attack in December 1944. If he had been caught by partisans, he would have suffered the same fate as his Duce. Marinetti had spent the last twenty years making the argument that Mussolini and Fascism were quintessentially modern, revolutionary, and, in a word, Futurist. It was only fitting that the Fascist regime, and Futurism, should thus perish simultaneously.

---

[41] F.T. Marinetti, "Risposta del poeta Marinetti agli scrittori Jules Romains-Duhamel-Benjamin Cremieux-Pierard-Ludwig Wolf-Wells," in *Il Giornale d'Italia*, July 12, 1940, found in Getty Research Center, Letters to Angelo Rognoni and One of His Manuscripts, 1914-1957, accession #850150, Box 2, Folder 4: Marinetti and Benedetta, 1916-1946.

The "Politica dei Ponti" in the Republic of Salò

William M. Adams

The relationship between Italian culture and fascism has been studied for the most part in the context of the fascist *ventennio*, the twenty-year regime that came to an end in the summer of 1943, with comparatively little attention being paid to how Italian culture interacted with fascism during its final phase under German occupation. Historians tend to dismiss this period as unworthy of scholarship, depicting it in rather monolithic terms as fascism's most extreme phase, although admittedly with some good reasons: because the Nazis had the final word in Italy, because the new Italian government was made up mostly of extremists and pro-Nazi elements, and most importantly, because the Holocaust was extended to Italy.

On July 26, 1943, Mussolini was ousted by the Fascist Grand Council and, on the king's orders, arrested and placed in secret confinement. Six weeks later the Germans discovered his whereabouts, rescued him and flew him first to Germany to confer personally with Hitler, then returned him to Italy as the head of a new regime called the Italian Social Republic, soon to be more popularly known as the Republic of Salò–"republic" because Italy was no longer a kingdom, since the royal family had fled to the Allied camp. The Germans quickly occupied the Italian peninsula as far south as Salerno.

On September 12, while still in Munich, Mussolini made a radio broadcast to Italy announcing his imminent return, in which he spelled out how this new fascist republic would differ from its predecessor regime. Fascism was to be renewed; it was to be re-established on the basis of the Italian working classes; "going back to our origins," as he phrased it, in order "to make labor the theme of our economy and the indestructible basis of the State."[1] By announcing labor as the new social basis of the Fascist Party, he intended to punish and exclude the Italian bourgeoisie,

---

[1] Quoted in F.W. Deakin, *The Brutal Friendship: Mussolini, Hitler, and the Fall of Italian Fascism* (New York/Evanston: Harper & Row, 1962), 565.

which he felt had turned against him and had proved uncooperative during the war. Most importantly, he believed socialism would win popular consensus for the new political arrangements. Scholars have found little that was genuine in Mussolini's socialization initiatives, however, seeing in them little more than a cynical attempt to take the wind out of the sails of the communists and woo the industrial working classes over to his side.

A renewed fascism was also very much in the minds of the extremists who led the propaganda ministry, the Ministry of Popular Culture, known as Minculpop. But their ideas were the opposite of Mussolini's; they envisioned fascism evolving in a more authoritarian and extremist direction. In this paper I will examine the role played by a few intellectuals whom Mussolini appointed as newspaper editors during the Salò Republic. With Mussolini's connivance, these editors ignored whenever possible official press directives in order to create an image of fascism distinctly at variance with that projected by the Salò propaganda ministry. I find the way Mussolini used the press was in fact analogous to his attempts to socialize Italian industry: both were meant to create the image of a renewed fascism, and both endeavors put him at odds with his own ministers and with the occupying Germans.

My work is based on research conducted under the supervision of the late and sorely missed Philip Cannistraro, whose first book, *La fabbrica del consenso*, must still be regarded as the starting point for understanding how fascism established a system for organizing and supervising culture on behalf of its political goals.[2] Research by other scholars in the years since its publication has largely confirmed what Cannistraro revealed about the nature of this system, and was recently summed up in the words of historian Ruth Ben-Ghiat as "a complex patronage structure that was designed to contain dissent and draw creative individuals into collaborative relationships with the state."[3]

Of the two main factors which have impeded the emergence of a substantial historiography on Salò, the most detrimental has been the political polarization lasting throughout most of the post-war period. What was written on the topic during these years is so divided along ideological lines that a true dialogue between historians is only now beginning to

---

[2] Philip V. Cannistraro, *La fabbrica del consenso. Fascismo e mass media* (Rome: Laterza, 1975).
[3] Ruth Ben-Ghiat, *Fascist Modernities. Italy, 1922-1945* (Berkeley/Los Angeles: University of California Press, 2001), 9.

emerge. A secondary problem—the deliberate and wholesale destruction of archival sources by members compromised by their own involvement—still makes it difficult to track down sources. Contributing to historians' distaste for the topic, there is the large (and still growing) body of literature published by Salò's adherents, who seek to legitimize the Salò Republic and rehabilitate fascism. Writing to justify their commitment to Salò, these authors voice no regrets for having staked everything on the Axis cause and offer no re-evaluation of Mussolini's dictatorship. The Holocaust, as well as the many German massacres of Italian civilians, go unmentioned.

The first comprehensive history of Salò appeared in 1962, when British historian F.W. Deakin wrote *The Brutal Friendship: Hitler, Mussolini, and the Fall of Italian Fascism*.[4] Deakin's work focuses primarily on German-Italian relations, and tends to uphold a rather generalized conception of Salò: that it was merely a puppet regime, or a "rump dictatorship" overwhelmingly influenced by Nazi domination. Yet Deakin identifies what he regards as its central issue, when he observes that "the only real asset of the republican regime was its labor force, the ultimate control of which was the only source of political power" vis-à-vis the Germans. "Should this," he asked, "be controlled by a civilian bureaucracy, by the machinery of the Party, by the new Republican Army . . . or by the Germans themselves?"[5] If control of the working classes was really the "central issue," a fascist government genuinely popular with the working classes would be the one that could most effectively bargain with the Germans.

It was not until the 1970s that there began to appear works departing from generalized, monolithic views of Salò, to present, instead, a series of conflicts between moderates and extremists. Recent research has overwhelmingly followed this trend, most notably with Lutz Klinkhammer's *L'occupazione tedesca in Italia*,[6] and Luigi Ganapini's *La Repubblica delle camicie nere*.[7] Renzo DeFelice died before his multi-volume biography of Mussolini got past the spring of 1944, although he discusses the first stage

---

[4] Ibid.

[5] Deakin, 667.

[6] Lutz Klinkhammer, *L'occupazione tedesca in Italia, 1943-1945* (Torino: Bollati Boringheri, 1996).

[7] Luigi Ganapini, *La repubblica delle camicie nere: i combattenti, i politici, gli amministratori, i socializzatori* (Milano: Garzanti, 1999).

of the "conciliation" or "pacification" campaign, soon to be known as the Politica dei ponti.[8]

The Politica dei ponti is a term that refers to the politics of building bridges between political divides. It began during the last days of the regime, a full month before Mussolini's ouster in July 1943, when neo-idealist philosopher Giovanni Gentile was asked by the Fascist Party secretary to explain the "historic, moral and legal reasons" behind Italy's involvement in the war; Gentile answered with a radio address broadcast from Rome's Campidoglio, the *Discorso agli italiani*.[9] This marks the inaugural moment of his "pacification of souls" campaign. Gentile's approach sought to annul the political differences among Italians by erecting a myth of national community based not on politics, but on culture. This effort necessarily involved a re-elaboration of the meaning of fascism in highly personal—and highly reductive—terms, distancing it from the authoritarianism of the past twenty years. Traditional motifs in fascist propaganda would now cast Italians in a different light, less the heirs of the warlike, conquering Romans, than as heirs of the Romans, who were the true builders of civilization, teachers of barbarians, and propagators of the gospel. Gentile emphasized such Roman virtues as discipline, concord, resolution in combat, and honor as the qualities Italians must find within themselves in order to face the impending invasion, which could only be won by uniting civilized Italians against the barbarian "other."

Such a rhetorical strategy must have made an impression on Mussolini; months after the July coup and his rescue by the Germans, he reached out to Gentile. The dictator arranged to have the philosopher appointed as head of the Accademia d'Italia as well as editor in chief of Italy's most prestigious periodical, the *Nuova Antologia*. In doing this, he provided an institutional basis for Gentile's pacification campaign to continue, even under German occupation. Everything Gentile wrote and spoke publicly from then until his assassination in April of the following year called for the "pacification of souls" and conciliation between Italians on the basis of their shared cultural heritage, all without complaint from the Duce.[10]

---

[8] Renzo De Felice, *Mussolini l'alleato. La guerra civile 1943-1945* (Torino: Einaudi, 1997).

[9] Benedetto Gentile, ed., *Giovanni Gentile. La vita e il pensiero. Dal Discorso alla morte* (Firenze: Sansoni, 1951).

[10] Gabriele Turi, *Giovanni Gentile. Una biografia* (Firenze: Giunti Gruppo Editore, 1995), 510-511.

Once Mussolini was back in Italy, and with the republican government founded under German auspices, he faced a new cabinet not of his own choosing, composed of men known to historians as the Intransigents. These were figures selected from a list drawn up by the German ambassador, Rudolf von Rahn. After securing their adherence, the new party secretary, Alessandro Pavolini, presented the final roster to Mussolini.[11] Besides Pavolini, the list included Roberto Farinacci, the notorious *ras* from Cremona, who ran the most fascist of newspapers, *Il Regime Fascista*, and Giovanni Preziosi, the most fanatical anti-Semite in the Italian press. Preventive censorship was relaxed, and lip service paid to the right of citizens to responsible criticism.[12]

Immediately after convening his first council of ministers, Mussolini turned his attention to the press, purging all the editors of the major newspapers and replacing them with new ones well known and loyal to him personally.[13] At once, the tendency of which Gentile proved the forerunner became virtually characteristic of these editors—an attempt to personally redefine fascism in a more tolerant, humane and even liberal direction. As soon as newspapers began to republish in the autumn of 1943 a remarkably free debate began to take shape—remarkable given the historical circumstances of a government bent on taking revenge. The questions that arose were: how much freedom of the press was to be tolerated? How far were writers permitted to go in discussing the flaws of fascism, of Mussolini, of the aims of the war? It goes without saying that no discussion of this sort ever took place in the two other totalitarian societies of Nazi Germany and the Soviet Union, and it went well beyond the cultural debates that appeared in various periodicals in the late 1930s, when fascism was subtly criticized in coded language. Even though he "officially" barely condoned discussion, Mussolini selected these editors and allowed the debate to continue. Furthermore, Mussolini himself advanced various lines of thought in the debate and, under a pseudonym (Giramondo), contributed to the discussion.[14]

---

[11] Deakin, 566.

[12] De Felice, 610.

[13] Silvio Bertoldi, *Salò. Vita e morte della Repubblica Sociale Italiana* (Milano: RCS Libri e Grande Opere, 1976), 292.

[14] Guglielmo Salotti, "Un 'mistero' storico-giornalistico: 'Il giramondo'." *Storia contemporanea*, 17.5 (October 1986), 875.

The Intransigents reacted with outrage at the idea that anyone should be allowed to criticize fascism. They intended to purify fascism of unreliable elements and political compromises, to render it even more absolutist and extreme, and their ideal for its evolution was Nazi Germany. They blamed the collapse on a conspiracy of corrupt *gerarchi* and the monarchy; fascism itself was blameless. One of the first negative reactions voiced against pacification came in early October 1943, when party secretary Pavolini instructed party federations to take a stand against it. Ten days later Propaganda Minister Fernando Mezzasoma issued a directive objecting to any further appeals that called for the "pacification of souls, concord of spirits, [and] the brotherhood of Italians," urging the press instead to exhort its readers to struggle and sacrifice at the side of the Germans. On November 5 Pavolini issued orders that "moral instigators" of partisan violence, by which he meant anyone calling for conciliation and discussion, be arrested each time a Fascist Party official was killed. Without the protection offered by Mussolini, Gentile would undoubtedly have been silenced by these extremists; Pavolini pointed him out as "one of the traitors" and Farinacci called him a "cheap opportunist."[15]

The Conciliators (as they came to be called) stayed the course. One of these, Ermanno Amicucci, the editor of Milan's *Corriere della sera*, published four articles in late November 1943 which dared to explore the causes of the country's collapse. This he did by summarizing arguments advanced by various readers who had written to the newspaper to express their opinions on the subject. The anger this provoked among the Intransigents was the likely reason behind Mussolini's issuance of a "clarification" on freedom of the press. Yet Amicucci was neither removed from his post nor arrested.[16]

The following month, Giorgio Pini, editor of Bologna's daily *Il Resto del Carlino*, began to run a series of editorials suggesting that the betrayal by the monarchy could only have taken place in an atmosphere created by the errors of fascism. Writing after the war, he claimed his intent was to persuade the political leadership to establish a system of accountability to the public, even that Italy should cease being a one-party state.[17] This stance may owe something to post-war self-justification; nevertheless the

---

[15] Ermano Amicucci, *I sei cento giorni di Mussolini: dal Gran Sasso a Dongo* (Rome: Faro, 1948), 123.

[16] Amicucci, 49.

[17] Giorgio Pini, *Itinerario tragico* (Milano: Edizioni Omnia, 1950).

articles Pini published in *Il Resto del Carlino* do relentlessly target authoritarianism. On December 5 he named fascism's greatest flaw as "the lack of public criticism."[18] A month later, he wrote "absolute authoritarianism, with its relative psychological separation between those who command and those who obey, along with the cold dogmatism that prevents a circulation of ideas, constitute errors we cannot allow ourselves to commit again."[19] Pini never shrank from presenting himself as a true fascist, an Italian patriot, a loyal supporter of Mussolini, nevertheless his writings encouraged his compatriots to envision a fascist government without authoritarianism. What about "believe, obey, fight"? What about *"il Duce ha sempre ragione"*? The loyal fascist Pini, who spoke personally with Mussolini every week, seemed to have been in conflict with some of the foundational values of fascism. His editorials prompted nothing worse than an official reprimand at Minculpop headquarters.[20]

Pini's increasingly urgent tone reached a climax in early April, with the publication of his most outspoken article, "Scongelare" [Thaw]. Describing a rally on behalf of an assassinated fascist militia chief, Pini noted the assembly's praise of their fallen comrade as a different kind of fascist, one who harbored a critical spirit, a nonconformist who believed in the young. Pini's own praise of these virtues begs the question: what did he think fascism was? As we saw with Gentile, Pini's is a decidedly reductive version of fascism expressed in personal and idiosyncratic terms; fascists, he eventually said, are "men who always do their duty as Italians, who live and struggle for the common good, for a free and powerful homeland, for an ideal of civilization and justice."[21] This vague definition could have included just about every patriotic Italian. Nowhere is there a hint of Roman martial valor, the "ethical state," superiority to liberal democracy and socialism, nor any of the blood-soaked imagery favored by the Intransigents, which formed the leitmotif of Salò propaganda.

Pini's articles provoked a display of strong public approval in the form of hundreds of letters sent to him—all anonymously. "Scongelare" earned him his second official admonishment from Minculpop. His last word on the subject was to write that "to obey and to fight, one must first believe." Six more months were to elapse, however, before he was re-

---

[18] Giorgio Pini, "Impostazione," *Il Resto del Carlino*, December 5, 1943.
[19] Giorgio Pini, "La terza strada," *Il Resto del Carlino*, January 10, 1944.
[20] Pini, *Itinerario*, 54.
[21] Giorgio Pini, "Scongelare," *Il Resto del Carlino*, April 2, 1944.

moved from the directorship of *Il Resto del Carlino* to become an undersecretary of the Interior, reporting to Mussolini himself.[22]

The Politica dei ponti campaign came to an end in late May 1944 with the reinstitution of preventive censorship—yet with one highly exceptional encore, when Concetto Pettinato, the editor of Turin's *La Stampa*, published an article entitled "Se ci sei, batti un colpo" [If you're there, give a knock]. Assigned as the editor of Turin's largest circulating daily, Pettinato entered the discussion by arguing that if the government truly wanted Italians to rally behind Salò's purified fascism, a new attitude towards freedom of discussion and criticism must be permitted.[23] After Minculpop made it clear that such sentiments were unwelcome, he held his peace until April. In the wake of Pini's "Scongelare," though, Pettinato returned to the topic of political freedom, insisting fascism adopt a "regular and constant contact, a cordial collaboration between authority and public."[24] Two weeks later, he called for an "intense political life, a real commitment, inspired by a clear vision . . . not blind obedience," and insisted it was necessary to change the reigning atmosphere within the party, with its aversion to all criticism.[25] Finally, in June of 1944, two weeks after the Allied capture of Rome and the Normandy landings, he published "Se ci sei, batti un colpo," a direct challenge to the government and to Mussolini. Nothing printed during the Salò Republic provoked as much excitement in the Italian public, or alarm in fascist and Nazi authorities, as this article. Rather than merely calling for freedom of the press, Pettinato boldly and confidently exercised it, speaking obvious truths about what the public already knew. He addressed the central weakness of the Salò Republic the alienation of its citizens–doing so by evaluating Salò as honestly and as brutally as anything found in the clandestine press of the Resistance or broadcast on Radio London. The alienation was not hard to explain, he said. The Salò government presented no tangible reality. It offered no security against partisan violence. Its socialization program was an obvious fraud. He questioned whether any Italian government really existed; was there anything behind the façade? "If you're there, give a knock." A government which gave its citizens nothing,

---

[22] Pini, *Itinerario*, 76.

[23] Concetto Pettinato, "Libertà e responsabilità," *La Stampa*, December 31, 1943. See also Concetto Pettinato, *Tutto da rifare* (Milano: Ceschina, 1966).

[24] Concetto Pettinato, "Incontrarci," *La Stampa*, April 7, 1944.

[25] Concetto Pettinato, "Critica e collaborazione," *La Stampa*, April 21, 1944.

meanwhile never ceasing to demand they throw away their lives for the sake of the country's honor, ought to be replaced, he said, by something that might offer hope.[26]

The German censor who allowed Pettinato's article to appear was promptly fired, but Minculpop's authorities raised no objections. Its publication caused an avalanche of support and serious consternation from the Intransigents and the Germans, who condemned it as disastrous and demoralizing. Pettinato immediately tendered his resignation, which was answered a few hours later by a refusal of its acceptance from Minculpop. He was allowed to continue editing *La Stampa*, but his "punishment" was being forbidden to publish editorials for several months. When advised to go into hiding a few weeks before the war ended, Pettinato said, years later, "I always had, I don't know why, complete faith in Mussolini's sentiments towards me."[27]

Much of the story related here is already known to historians and can be found in the autobiographies of some of the key personalities involved, as well as the newspapers and periodicals of the time. Writing during the 1970s, some historians bring up the story of "Se ci sei, batti un colpo," but endow it with little significance. At the very least, the Politica dei ponti is worth noting as an exercise in fascist self-presentation, whose significance lies in the light it sheds on Mussolini's obviously negative attitude towards his government's propaganda, not to mention his own ministers. The editors he appointed constituted, in a sense, a kind of shadow propaganda ministry that worked in opposition to the Ministry of Popular Culture. The Politica dei ponti deserves to be more fully integrated within an overall history of Salò because it shows how Mussolini tried to reposition himself within the power structure of the new government, and demonstrates, just as his socialist initiatives did, how he imagined he might rebuild a popular consensus among people weary of war and occupation. Mussolini's attempt to undermine the extremist, purified version of fascism which emanated from Minculpop to instead give Italians something more appealing suggests he might have shared Deakin's assessment: controlling the labor supply was the key issue, the key to power, for any government that tried to rule Italy; whoever could do that would best be able to bargain with the occupying Germans. The kind

---

[26] Concetto Pettinato, "Se ci sei, batti un colpo," *La Stampa*, June 21, 1944.
[27] Pettinato, *Tutto*, 315-318.

of propaganda produced by Minculpop might have appealed to die-hard fanatics, but it was unlikely to gain Mussolini the kind of mass following he would need to bargain with Hitler. Suspecting his countrymen wanted socialism, and learning how much they yearned for freedom of discussion, he set about providing them with an illusion of what they wanted.

The illusory quality of this endeavor must certainly be emphasized. In truth, the attempt to present fascism as more tolerant, liberal or humane took place only among a few figures chosen personally by Mussolini. It was, aside from Gentile's *Discorso*, a tightly controlled propaganda ploy directed from above, something ex-newspaper editors and dictators are good at. No real freedom of discussion ever emerged in the Salò Republic. If Mussolini had been interested in granting such freedom, such debates would have included far more people and been much more extensive. The Politica dei ponti episode illustrates, one last time in his political life, Mussolini's cynical instinct to divide and rule by creating the illusion of consent, by orchestrating the works of writers and intellectuals for his own benefit. Such efforts during fascism's final hours confirms that this was a technique of exploitation he could not let go of—even at the end, even with the world falling down around his ears.

WRESTLING WITH TWO ANGELS:
COMMUNISM AND CHRISTIANITY IN THE WORK OF IGNAZIO SILONE

Stanislao G. Pugliese

It is not often that an author has an opportunity to revisit with his readers an earlier work, but this collection of essays in honor of Phil Cannistraro* affords an occasion to rethink the Italian writer Ignazio Silone's tormented relationship with two competing ideologies: orthodox Catholicism and orthodox Marxism.[1] His struggle offers a prism through which students and scholars of Italian studies might engage the workings of Catholicism and Marxism in Italy during the 20th century.

"Ignazio Silone" was born in 1923 in a Spanish prison. Perhaps it was no coincidence–and surely appropriate–that at the time he was reading Dostoevsky.[2] Secondino Tranquilli, the person whose identity he erased with his new name, had been born twenty three years earlier in the rural Abruzzo region of Italy and burdened with the given name "Secondino" which, in the local dialect, meant "prison guard." In Spain, he had been writing for Andrés Nin's journal *La Batalla* and imprisoned as a communist. Significantly, he derived "Silone" from the ancient warrior Poppedius Silo, a native of Silone's beloved Abruzzo. Silo had led a successful revolt against the tyranny of Rome in 90 B.C. and thereby gained official recognition of the local population's autonomy. "Ignazio" he borrowed from the Spanish Counter-Reformation saint Loyola and was chosen by Silone to "baptize the pagan surname."[3] In this defiant act of self-

---

* I did not have the good fortune to study with Phil; he started at the CUNY Graduate School just as I was finishing a dissertation on Giustizia e Libertà with Frank Rosengarten, John Cammett, Mary Gibson, Daniel Gasman and Bernard Semmel.

[1] Parts of this essay have previously appeared in *Bitter Spring: A Life of Ignazio Silone*. (New York: Farrar, Straus and Giroux, 2009). I thank publisher Jonathan Galassi for permission to reprint.

[2] "Primo incontro con Dostoievski," in *La Fiera Letteraria*, March 4, 1956; reprinted in, *Ignazio Silone. Romanzi e saggi*, edited by Bruno Falcetto (Milan: Mondadori, 1998-99) [*ISRS*], vol. 2, 1244-46.

[3] *Il pane di casa*, edited by Giuseppe Ardrizzo (Bergamo: Minerva Italia, 1971); quoted in Bruno Falcetto, "Cronologia," in *ISRS*, vol. 1, p. lxxv.

appellation and identity-creation, he thereby synthesized a classical, pagan past with the Christian tradition.

Silone has most often been associated with the protagonist of his novels *Bread and Wine* and *The Seed Beneath the Snow*, Pietro Spina. ("Read my books," he once said, "only in them do I fully recognize myself.") A communist intellectual and activist, Spina is returning from exile to his native Abruzzo, hunted by the fascist police. In order to elude arrest and move about the countryside, he dons the robes of a priest and becomes Don [Father] Paolo Spada. The metamorphosis from Pietro Spina (literally Peter [the] Thorn) to Paolo Spada (Paul [the] Sword) is revealing: The communist "thorn" is transformed into the religious "sword." The American literary critic Edmund Wilson, after reading Silone's novels sitting on the benches of the Villa Borghese Gardens in Rome, Italian dictionary at his side, perceptively sensed that Silone was "a queer mixture of priest and communist."[4] Nicola Chiaromonte, Silone's fellow founder and editor of the literary-cultural journal *Tempo Presente*, and one of the few people who could claim to be close to the writer, intuited that Silone was in some ways a *"prete contadino,"* a peasant priest.[5]

Yet Silone's life and experience is reflected in many of his characters, not just Pietro Spina/Paolo Spada. There is the peasant Berardo Viola in *Fontamara*, Thomas the Cynic in *The School for Dictators*, the disillusioned party intellectual Rocco De Donatis in *A Handful of Blackberries*, the doggedly persistent Andrea Cipriani in *The Secret of Luca*, the compassionate Daniele of *The Fox and the Camelias*, self-effacing Pope Celestine V in *The Story of a Humble Christian*. But there is always a clear, explicit and sincere identification with the poor Christ, the suffering Christ, the peasant Christ who figures in the mythology of the rural poor. And in his last, unfinished work, *Severina*, Silone for the first and only time identifies himself with a female protagonist. Severina, a young convent initiate who refuses to give false testimony in court even though ordered to do so by her Mother Superior, grew out of Silone's fascination at the end of his life with Simone Weil. A member of the French underground, a writer, and Jew who died by self-starvation in 1943, Weil inspired Silone to create

---

[4] Silone at the time was teaching Wilson Italian in post-war Rome. Lewis M. Dabney, *Edmund Wilson: A Life in Literature* (New York: Farrar, Straus and Giroux, 2005), 321-22.

[5] Nicola Chiaromonte, "Silone il rustico," in *Il Mondo* 1952.

Severina as bystander to a crime, thus embodying what writing meant for him: "the absolute necessity of bearing witness."[6]

Representativeness was imposed on Silone, wrote R. W. B. Lewis in a profile that, now almost a half century old, is still the best critical analysis of the writer.[7] "He scarcely had a chance to be Italian." Further complicating his portrait is the essential paradox that defined him: his entrance into politics because of an essentially religious conception of the world. "He became a socialist," Lewis writes, "because he wanted to become a saint."[8] As a priest says of one of Silone's characters, "socialism was his way of serving God."[9]

Silone is a particularly difficult subject for the biographer because of the labyrinthine meanderings of his own identity and his enigmatic autobiographical comments. He believed that the true nature of any person could not be known because–following the Neapolitan philosopher Giambattista Vico–he insisted that man is not nature. "Every man," he wrote, "is much more complicated than what he appears and that which he believes himself to be . . . to hell with psychology and facile suppositions."[10]

Did Silone knowingly encourage a misreading and a conflation of his heroic and morally pure main characters with his own biography? Is it true, as others now insist, that Silone offered a confession for his transgressions as a police spy in a minor protagonist? The transfiguration from Secondino Tranquilli to Ignazio Silone was neither the first nor the last of his many self-transformations.

When I asked Silone's widow about his fate in Italian literary circles and why no biography on him had been written in English, Darina Silone replied "That situation was Silone's own fault; his–to say the least–extremely difficult character."[11] When I noted the difficulty in tracking

---

[6] "Emergency Exit," in *Emergency Exit*, translated by Harvey Fergusson II (New York: Harper & Row, 1968), 46.

[7] Silone wrote the American critic that "in the future, your essay will constitute an indispensable source of consultation for whoever wishes to understand my work." Silone to Lewis, July 5, 1961, Archivio Silone, Florence, busta 3, fascicolo 23.

[8] "Ignazio Silone: The Politics of Charity," in *The Picaresque Saint* (Philadelphia: Lippincott, 1956), 113, 121.

[9] *Bread and Wine* in *The Abruzzo Trilogy*, translated by Eric Mosbacher, revised by Darina Silone (South Royalton, VT: Steerforth Press, 2000), 438.

[10] Quoted by Bruno Falcetto, "Introduzione," in *ISRS*, vol. 1, pp. xxxiii, xxxiv.

[11] Personal correspondence, letter of August 11, 2000.

down documents in the various archives and trying to fashion an identity from them, she was quick to respond: "There are things that are not found in any archive," she insisted. "Silone's character was difficult; his personality very complex. Of the few people alive who knew him personally, I am perhaps the one who knew him best, even if certainly not completely (no one ever knew him completely)."[12]

Where, exactly, does identity lie? Talcott Parson's "looking glass" theory ("I am not who I think I am; I am not who you think I am; I am who I think you think I am"), doesn't help us in Silone's case for he simply did not care what others in the Italian political and literary establishment thought of him. But the biographer has a fertile mine in Silone's own writings. Rarely has an *oeuvre* been so autobiographical. All of Silone's novels except one take place in the Abruzzo region of Italy, as do his two plays. Rarely has so cosmopolitan a writer been so closely identified with the place of his birth. "Look at Silone," said Albert Camus, noting the paradox in an interview after winning the Nobel Prize in Literature, "he is radically tied to his land but is the most European of writers . . . Silone speaks to all of Europe. If I feel myself tied to him it is because he is incredibly rooted in his national and even local tradition."[13] Not that Silone engaged in any sentimental or nostalgic myth-making of his origins. Indeed, one is struck by his complicated and ambivalent relationship with his hometown of Pescina. Notwithstanding all the autobiographical detail in his work, the problem of uncovering his identity still remains almost insurmountable for the biographer. "There is no single truth about Silone," Darina Silone once said, "only many truths."[14]

The writing is deceptively simple and presents the biographer with multiple challenges. Silone recognized himself in Hugo von Hofmannsthal's dictum that writers are a human category for whom writing is more difficult than it is for anyone else. "I live in a close communion with the characters in my stories that cannot be broken from one day to the next," Silone once wrote. So close was that identification that the necessity of

---

[12] Ibid. *"nessuno l'ha mai conosciuto a fondo"* (Darina had originally spoken these sentiments at the centenary celebrations of Silone's birth, May 1, 2000, in Pescina).

[13] Interview in the Parisian weekly *Demain*, November 15, 1957, 21.

[14] Peter Coleman, "Ignazio Silone," *Quadrant* vol. XLVIII, n. 1 (January 2004).

actually finishing a book was "an arbitrary and painful act, an act against nature, at any rate, my nature."[15]

The flawed, tragic hero is only one possible trope in crafting a biography of Silone. Like an ancient Hebrew prophet or one of the early persecuted Christians, Silone insisted on a moral vision of the world. His writing–"bearing witness"–was to become the testimony of an age. This is related to what might be called "the Christian quandary" or Silone's "wrestling with the Lord." He refused to take the more facile path of an easy atheism or agnosticism. Christianity for Silone was both a historical movement, tied to a certain place and time, and a transcendent, timeless moral force. This conflicting tension between an adamant historicism and a desire for transcendence are ever-present in his thought and writing. Silone and his main protagonists are not so much searching for a hidden God as being hounded by the Lord. A doggedly persistent deity haunts Silone and his characters, seeking them out in desolate landscapes and humble farmhouses, donkey stalls and empty churches. The moral and ethical impetus is more St. Augustine's *Confessions* than Beckett's *Waiting for Godot*. There is, as Irving Howe noted, an irreducible tension in all of Silone's writings between the secular promise of socialist liberation and the Christian promise of spiritual transcendence.[16] Despite his identification with both Christianity and socialism, Silone indelibly defined himself as "a Socialist without a Party, a Christian without a Church."[17]

Silone was honest enough to recognize the potential and contemporary failure of the Catholic Church just as he fearlessly recognized the potential and failure of orthodox Marxism. There was no Dantean, "comedic" vision of Christianity in Silone; he confessed to being an "absurd Christian." Theologically, orthodox Christianity can not accept absurdity or nihilism, yet for Silone, these must be confronted before they can be transcended. For Silone, the promise of Christianity as embodied in the Easter Resurrection has not come to pass. Instead, for the peasants of southern Italy–indeed for peasants and workers around the world–it is, he insisted, still–and always–Good Friday. While the writer felt himself hounded by the Lord, Silone's peasants ask, like Christ on the cross, "My

---

[15] See Silone's "Note on the Revision of *Fontamara*" in *Fontamara*, translated by Eric Mosbacher. (London: J. M. Dent & Sons, Ltd., 1985), xi.

[16] Irving Howe, Introduction to Ignazio Silone, *Bread and Wine*, translated by Eric Mosbacher (New York: New American Library, 1988), v-vi.

[17] Interview in *L'Express*, Paris, January 23, 1961.

God, my God, why have you abandoned me?" Surely the most anguished and–for the Christian–the most disturbing line in the Bible.

Nor could Marxism offer salvation or redemption. In an early work he once concluded: "The future belongs to Socialism." Years later, he repudiated that sentiment and the entire work in which it was written and strictly forbade its re-printing.[18] Just as he could not bring himself to simply accept a comedic teleology of Christianity, he eventually came to question and then reject Marxist eschatology and teleology.

William Faulkner thought him Italy's greatest living writer, and intellectuals as diverse as Thomas Mann, Albert Camus, Graham Greene, and Edmund Wilson agreed. Yet even his most astute readers, focused on his moral and political seriousness, often fail to note Silone's irony and humor. He once wrote that since pathos cannot be eliminated from human life, "a touch of irony is required to make it acceptable."[19] Silone's irony could indeed be bitter but it was always moderated by a critical spirit and an independence of judgment. Although tragedy and sorrow were inherent in the human condition—he often wrote of "our inhuman fate upon the earth"[20]—there remained the possibility of hope. His politics could be described as a humanistic socialism, combined with a compassionate libertarianism. He was an admirer of the anarchists Pierre-Joseph Proudhon, Peter Kropotkin, and Camillo Berneri (the last assassinated by Stalin's agents during the Spanish Civil War). When Berneri's widow, Giovanna, in her journal *Volontà*, implied that Silone was an anarchist, the writer wrote her a letter in response in which he said he would be honored to be counted in their number, if only to distinguish himself from the various

---

[18] Ignazio Silone, *Der Fascismus: seine Entstehung und seine Entwicklung* (Zurich: Europa Verlag, 1934). In spite of Silone's clear instructions that the book was not to be translated into Italian, it appeared as *Il fascismo. Origini e sviluppo* (Carnago: SugarCo Edizioni, 1992) and, most recently, edited by Mimmo Franzinelli (Milan: Mondadori, 2002). Speaking of this last version, Darina Silone, the writer's widow, wrote that "Franzinelli has done a really splendid job." When asked about the possibility of an English translation, she noted that a British publisher was interested but that she hoped they would not move forward as "it couldn't possibly be nearly as good as the Mondadori edition." Personal correspondence, Darina Silone to the author, July 7, 2002.

[19] "Author's Note" (1962) to *Bread and Wine* in *The Abruzzo Trilogy*, 180.

[20] Letter to Girolamo Valenti meant as a preface to a 1936 American edition of *Fontamara*, that, for unknown reasons, was never published. The original letter is today archived in the Taminent Institute of New York University and published by Sergio Bugiardini in *Ignazio Silone. Clandestino del novecento*, edited by Luce d'Eramo (Rimini: Editori Riminesi, 1996), 146-48.

forms of socialism then current in Italy. "But a great respect toward those who have studied, struggled and suffered to give the anarchist ideal a precise shape" prevented him from identifying himself as such.[21] Nine years later, in a sympathetic response to the student uprisings of 1968, Silone commented that "democracy has a duty to respect utopia."

By nature silent, meditative and melancholy, Silone belied the stereotype of the gregarious, outgoing, extroverted southern Italian. In *The Seed Beneath the Snow*, a sympathetic character remarks to Pietro Spina's grandmother (modeled on Silone's own maternal grandmother): "There is a kind of sadness, a subtle kind of sadness that must not be confused with the more ordinary kind that's the result of remorse, disappointment, or suffering; there's a kind of intimate sadness and hopelessness that attaches itself for preference to chosen souls. . . . That kind of sadness has always been very prevalent among sensitive individuals in this part of the world. Once upon a time, to avoid suicide or madness, they entered monasteries."[22]

Unable or unwilling to enter a monastery, Silone gravitated to politics at an early age. But painfully shy, uncomfortable in the public light and perpetually doubtful of himself, Silone never had any of the qualities necessary for a successful political career. He was a difficult husband, an exasperating friend, a mediocre politician, an aloof acquaintance, a morose presence in public, a distant and cool relative, often manic-depressive, sometimes suicidal, and carried out an epistolary exchange with a police official that has now shadowed his reputation for the last decade. Yet, starting in the 1930s, he crafted a body of work that testifies to a searing political and spiritual crisis and still bears fruitful reading. Silone offers us today a critical commentary on everything that we as human beings have experienced in the twentieth century: from the failed promise of political utopia to the disillusionment with art; from the nihilism of totalitarianism to the moral temptations and seductive corruption of an affluent but savage, consumerist culture.

---

[21] Silone to Giovanna Berneri, February 11, 1959, Archivio Silone, Florence, busta 3, fascicolo 21.
[22] Don Severino speaking to Donna Maria Vincenza, *The Seed Beneath the Snow*, in *The Abruzzo Trilogy*, 590.

Curiously, Silone has never been the subject of a biography in English.[23] Even in Italy, when not neglected by the literary and cultural establishment, he was often the object of scorn and derision, accused of writing "bad Italian." Awash in a sea of hagiographical works, there is some discerning, insightful scholarship on Silone in Italian for the serious reader.[24] But considering the ethical dimensions of his writing and the wide range of his literary production, one might be surprised that his work has not attracted greater attention in America. While known mainly for his novels, Silone mastered the art of the essay (*Emergency Exit*), the theoretical treatise (*Fascism: Its Origins and Development*), political satire (*The School for Dictators*), as well as drama (*And He Hid Himself; The Story of a Humble Christian*). When *The School for Dictators* first appeared in 1938 (with dictators ascendant), Silone was acclaimed "a second Machiavelli" by some overly-enthusiastic critics, as, conversely, his *Manifesto for Civil Disobedience* of December 1942, in which he urges the peoples of Europe to rise up against the Fascist and Nazi dictatorships with non-violent public resistance, makes one think of Mahatma Gandhi and Dr. Martin Luther King, Jr.

Critics and readers of twentieth-century Italian literature are now familiar with the so-called "caso Silone" (Silone case), first broached in the postwar years: Why was Silone so beloved and read abroad and so neglected at home in Italy? It was only late in his life that the Italian literary establishment issued a collective *mea culpa* and showered Silone with lit-

---

[23] Two important studies should be mentioned here: Maria Nicolai Paynter's *Ignazio Silone: Beyond the Tragic Vision* (Toronto: University of Toronto Press, 2000) and Elizabeth Leake's *The Reinvention of Ignazio Silone* (Toronto: University of Toronto Press, 2003). The first is not a biography but a fine work of literary criticism. As will become apparent, although indebted to Paynter's work, I question whether Silone ever transcended the tragic vision of life. Leake's work is not a full fledged biography but a psychoanalytical reinterpretation of Silone in light of the charges that he spied for the fascist regime. Perhaps the best critical work on Silone in English remains "Ignazio Silone: The Politics of Charity" in R. W. B. Lewis's, *The Picaresque Saint:* Representative Figures in Contemporary Fiction (Philadelphia: Lippincott & Co., 1959).

[24] Two outstanding works, to which I am much indebted, are Luce d'Eramo, *L'opera di Ignazio Silone: Saggio critico e guida bibliografica* (Milan: Mondadori, 1971) and Bruno Falcetto's meticulous editing of Silone's collected works in two volumes as *Ignazio Silone. Romanzi e saggi* (Milan: Mondadori, 1998/1999). Also of immense help were Vittoriano Esposito, *Vita e pensiero di Ignazio Silone* (Cerchio: Adelmo Polla, 1993) and Diocleziano Giardini, *Ignazio Silone. Cronologia della vita e delle opere* (Cerchio: Adelmo Polla, 1999).

erary prizes. Robert Gordon has concisely delineated Silone's post-war critical reputation:

> Ironically, the foreign writers and critics who had championed Silone in the 1930s and 1940s as a great writer gradually lost interest in his later work, unable or unwilling to stomach his increasingly intense libertarian Christianity. For them Silone would always be a standard-bearer of the cause of anti-Fascism and of the necessity for moral enquiry in literature. As such, he was to be set alongside Camus, Koestler, Malraux, Orwell and others, and to be remembered principally for his earlier works, including *Fontamara*. Other critics more open to his later work did emerge, but in turn they tended to neglect *Fontamara*, where the themes of introspective morality and crisis are muted and poverty and politics are to the fore. They tried to fit Silone into another company of writers, of Christian moralists such as Bernanos, Péguy, and Greene. Despite their best efforts, however, it is undeniable that Silone's international reputation faded somewhat, along with that of the anti-Fascist or existentialist generation.[25]

By 1967, Iris Origo could write that admiration for Silone "has now become not only the fashion, but almost a certificate of integrity."[26] Almost as soon as Origo had penned these words, another "Silone affair" exploded when it was discovered that the Congress for Cultural Freedom, of which Silone was a leading member, and his beloved journal, *Tempo Presente*, were being indirectly financed by the Central Intelligence Agency with funds laundered through the Ford Foundation. Silone immediately resigned from the CCF and in 1968 closed down the journal, but the allegations that he was a spy for the CIA persisted. Documents from the National Archives in Washington, D.C., however, demonstrate that during World War II Silone was working with the OSS (Office of Strategic Services, forerunner of the CIA) in trying to overthrow fascism and establish democracy in Italy.[27] His fervent letters and telegrams depict a Silone who was desperate that the Italian people, victims of fascism

---

[25] Robert Gordon, "Silone and His Critics," in Ignazio Silone, *Fontamara* (London: J. M. Dent, 1994), 173.

[26] Iris Origo, *A Need to Testify* (San Diego: Harcourt Brace Jovanovich, 1984), 312.

[27] The documents have been reproduced by a Swiss scholar and are available online at www.peterkamber.ch/ignazio.html

for over twenty years, should not have to pay the price for the sins of Mussolini's regime. A careful reading of these documents reveals that Silone was no spy. It hardly seems likely that Silone was later a spy for the CIA when, despite the intervention of both Adlai Stevenson and Clare Booth Luce, he was denied a visa to visit the United States until the mid-1960s. (He had, during the Second World War, been offered asylum by no less a person than Eleanor Roosevelt.) In light of his beleaguered circumstances–denied by both the Right and the Left–Silone was adopted by the democratic socialists of the United States and lauded by the intellectual and literary circles of *The Partisan Review*, *Dissent*, and *The Nation* and critics and writers such as Clement Greenberg, Alfred Kazin, Mary McCarthy and Irving Howe worked to bring his work to the attention of an American audience.

Slowly but surely Silone's reputation survived all these charges. After his death in 1978, it seemed that Silone's literary reputation was secured, especially after the distinguished publishing house Mondadori published much of Silone's oeuvre in its prestigious "Meridiani" series in two deluxe volumes. But over the last decade another "caso Silone" has darkened his reputation. In 1996, an Italian historian uncovered documents supposedly proving that Silone had been spying for the fascist secret police. Over the next few years, new revelations appeared in the press and academic journals. Apparently, Silone had spent nearly a decade in an epistolary exchange with a high-ranking police official in Rome. Once again, Silone was at the center of political, literary and cultural scandal.

This latest "caso Silone" did not arise in a vacuum. Silone had not been a stranger to controversy in life. Perhaps the ur-scandal was his class betrayal: for although he and his family were petit bourgeois, owning some properties in the Fucino plain of the Marsica region in the Abruzzo, he cast his lot with the *cafoni* all over the world in their myriad guises. As his alter ego Pietro Spina muses in a letter "perhaps the real cause of my distress is my defiance of the ancient law, my way of living in cafés, libraries, hotels, my having broken the chain that for centuries linked my forefathers to the soil."[28] Later, there followed another scandal in his expulsion from the Italian Communist Party (PCI) in 1931 and his subsequent exile in Switzerland. Although his 1933 novel, *Fontamara*, was a critical and commercial success, there was the scandal of his writing's

---

[28] *Bread and Wine* in *The Abruzzo Trilogy*, 260.

critical reception in Italy, where, upon returning from exile in 1944, he faced a domestic, literary ostracization that was no less devastating than his physical exile. For decades, the classically-trained literary establishment refused to countenance Silone's work. It was said that he didn't write "proper Italian." He was often passed over for major literary awards. His subject matter–the rural Abruzzo and the *cafoni*–were considered beneath "proper" literature by the conservative establishment while the cultural elites of the Left, dominated by the PCI, could not forget his expulsion from the party in 1931 nor forgive his criticism of communism during the Cold War. When his account of disillusionment with communism, "Emergency Exit," appeared in Richard Crossman's anthology *The God that Failed* in 1950, Silone was mercilessly criticized by his former comrades and when that essay became the central piece in an autobiographical volume, *Uscita di sicurezza* (*Emergency Exit*, 1965), the communist-dominated committee of the prestigious Viareggio Prize refused to accept it for consideration, thus generating further controversy (the book was awarded the Marzotto Prize instead). Italian critics began asking themselves why was it that Silone was so prized abroad and so derided at home. As the American scholar Michael P. McDonald has written, it was a classic case of *Nemo propheta acceptus est patria sua*.[29] Contemporary neo-fascists (or post-fascists as they like to fashion themselves) as well as paleo-communists are loath to forget Silone's "betrayal": his effective demolition of their precious and precarious myths.

The most recent scandal, that Silone was engaged in a decade-long spying operation against his comrades in the Italian Communist Party, has come to overshadow everything else, calling into question as it does Silone's status as a reluctant secular saint of the independent Left in Europe, a persona that Silone worked hard to root in the public imagination. In Silone's second novel, *Bread and Wine*, Don Benedetto reads from an old essay of Pietro Spina's: "But for the fact that it would be very boring to be exhibited on altars after one's death, to be prayed to and worshiped by a lot of unknown people, mostly ugly old women, I should like to be a saint."[30] But surely he would have echoed Doris Day's retort: "Don't call me a saint; I don't want to be dismissed so easily." And it was George Orwell, to whom Silone has often been compared, who wrote "saints

---

[29] "No prophet is accepted in his own country." Luke 4:24. See McDonald's essay on the most recent controversy, "Il Caso Silone," in *The National Interest*, Fall 2001, 77-89.

[30] *Bread and Wine*, in *The Abruzzo Trilogy*, 201.

should always be judged guilty until they are proved innocent,"[31] a sentiment that surely would have provoked a wry smile and a knowing nod from the Italian writer. "Silone was the man of capital letters," his wife recalled, "he used to write the word "verità" with a capital "V"; "libertà" with a capital "L." But his lower-case character was mysterious and unknowable."[32]

How then, in this tangled thicket of representation, self-representation and mis-representation, is a historian and biographer to approach Silone? And how should these most recent revelations affect our perception of the writer? Perhaps a comparison with an earlier work–also a biography[33]–might prove useful. Then, the subject (Carlo Rosselli), while a complex and charismatic figure, was a relatively "open" text, his thinking accessible through his essays, letters, anti-fascist activism, and most important theoretical work. Silone, by contrast, has almost only been "known" through an association with the protagonists of his novels and his autobiographical essays. But this presents the reader and biographer with a challenge. As Elizabeth Leake demonstrates in her recent analysis, Silone reinvented himself as a novelist who had passed through the inferno of the militant's life in the communist underground, thereby giving his writings an aura of authenticity. Because of his role as fascist informer, Leake argues that his identity was based on "incoherent decisions" and that when the discrepancies between his life and his fiction are taken into account, the reader is unable to fix Silone's position on the moral spectrum. "The paradoxical nature of his identity," she concludes, "is thus insurmountable."[34] But was Silone's transformation insincere and therefore, in some way, deceitful? There is no reason not to believe that Silone's transition from underground political activist to exiled, solitary writer was not as sincere and painful as he claimed.

Silone's notoriously difficult personality has sometimes been blamed on a certain strain of misanthropy. To the German writer Bernard von Brentano he wrote in May of 1936:

---

[31] "Reflections on Gandhi," in *Partisan Review*, January 1949.

[32] Darina Silone, *Colloqui*, 87-88.

[33] Stanislao G. Pugliese, *Carlo Rosselli: Socialist Heretic and Antifascist Exile* (Cambridge, MA: Harvard University Press, 1999).

[34] Leake, *The Reinvention of Ignazio Silone*, 7.

The difficulty Spina encounters (in *Bread and Wine*) in communicating with other men reflects in good measure my state of mind (*stato di anima*). Relations with other people do not have a simple, natural, and direct character which I would love. This dissatisfaction sometimes pushes me toward solitude and willful silence. It is not misanthropy, but just the opposite: a love of man that remains unsatisfied, a need for friendship that fails to find its subject. This ends by irritating me and wearing me out. I begin again to love solitude as I loved it when I was 17: it is a very particular kind of solitude in which one chooses and invents one's friends, and one reads much.[35]

My biography employs neither the psychoanalytical approach (for which I am not trained) nor the literary-critical method, for I am convinced that the "truth" of Silone's life lies neither hidden in the archives nor wholly revealed in his writings but in some contested and ambiguously mapped terrain between memoir, literature, and history.

That terrain was shaped by the forces of heresy in daring to challenge certain Marxist and Stalinist "truths," exile in Switzerland, and the twin tragedies of a failed politics and a disillusionment with the Catholic Church. In the 1920s, as a major figure of the international communist movement, Silone refused to accept the orthodoxy of Stalin's cult and suffered the fate of the heretic, excommunicated from the Marxist Church. Broken, disillusioned, told by his doctors that he was near death and contemplating suicide, Silone retreated to Davos, Switzerland where he began composing his most famous work, *Fontamara*, literally "Bitter Spring." The book's "unforeseen and unforeseeable" success "made me a writer," he recalled forty years later.[36] Like a long line of Italian intellectuals before him, from Dante to Machiavelli, from Mazzini to Garibaldi, exile transformed Silone into an entirely new person. He was ostracized by the communists and hunted by the fascists. Rather than the relatively congenial exile of bohemian Paris, Silone chose austere, Protestant Zurich. He was accused of failing to change with literary taste, of refusing to accommodate the whims of the reading public; of writing the same book over and over again. But as his close friend and colleague the Polish writer Gustaw Herling wrote about him, "Anyone who is deeply convinced that

---

[35] May 14, 1936, Zurich. Archivio Silone, Florence, busta 4, fascicolo 6.

[36] Silone to Mariapia Bonanate, January 1973, Archivio Silone, Florence, busta 10, fascicolo 1.

he is saying something important is not ashamed to say things more than once. The secret is the gravity of the words, and what gives words their gravity is their unceasing vigilance."[37] Herling, who had settled in Naples in 1955, would confide that Silone was "truly a man who kept secrets and did not speak much."[38]

It was this existential status as an outsider and exile—even after returning to Italy—that marked his life and work. An interviewer once noted a certain "Erasmian component" to his personality. But an Erasmus plucked from the aristocratic Renaissance and dropped into the industrial age, "not afraid to get his hands dirty in peasant revolts." This was an Erasmus which rendered Silone "a citizen of an invisible world community of free men, not very numerous, but united by cultural ties." This Italian had no homeland.[39] Indeed, Silone claimed no other citizenship except that of this "imagined communion" with peasants and workers around the world, so different from the "imagined communities" of nationalism.

Silone's personal traumas (the loss of his father, the death of his mother in an earthquake, his precarious physical and mental health, his brother's imprisonment and death, his "spying") inevitably left their marks but were only obliquely played out in his work. It was only the public trauma of expulsion from the PCI that was explicit in his writing. "There is a secret in my life," he once confessed in an interview, "it is written between the lines of my books."[40] His struggle with demons private and public may not have been as obvious as other intellectuals with whom he has often been compared, such as Sartre or Camus or Orwell, yet it was no less dramatic. His story is, in short, a modernist tragedy.

Silone represents a special genre of intellectual: passionately committed to a political ideology that eventually proves illusory; in the light of that failure desperately attempting not to succumb to nihilism; perhaps morally compromised by a relationship to the very powers of oppression; caught in a Sisyphean task of political liberation in a century that placed

---

[37] Gustaw Herling, "Rome, December 2" [Ignazio Silone] in *Volcano and Miracle: A Selection From the Journal Written at Night*, translated by Ronald Strom (New York: Penguin, 1996), 28.

[38] "L'avventura di un povero cristiano e di un povero socialista," in *ISRS*, vol. 1, xii.

[39] Interview with Ugo Alfassio Grimaldi in "Alcune domande a un francotiratore del socialismo," in *Critica Sociale*, November 20, 1965; reprinted in *ISRS*, vol. 2, 1273.

[40] Silone's interview was broadcast on Italian television, RaiEducational, "La Storia Siamo Noi," on February 28, 2004; I am indebted to Romolo Tranquilli for providing me with a videotaped copy of the program.

all the powers of modern mass communication, technology, and awesome violence in the hands of totalitarian states.

In 1962, Silone and his wife Darina made a pilgrimage of sorts to the Holy Land. They had taken the road from Jerusalem to Bethlehem and found themselves in a barren valley bereft of any trees, shrubs, plants or flowers. There was no sign of water or human life. But near Bethlehem they came upon a woman dressed all in black, carrying a child and riding a dusty, grey donkey. The three silent figures passed Silone and his wife without so much as a glance in their direction. The vision created in Silone a particular state of mind and he was silent for a long time. Although he had never been in this part of the world, he had the distinct impression that he had already seen and lived this panorama. It was Darina who after a long while broke the silence pointing out to her husband that this was the landscape of his novels. It was a revelation. "I saw once again, outside of myself, something that I had carried within me for years, perhaps since birth: the landscape of my soul."[41] In this landscape, bread, wine, wolves, donkeys, and water all held potent hold on his imagination, both in their literal and symbolic manifestations. Water in all its forms–from fountains and springs to snow and tears–is always critical in his work. (One is reminded of Picasso's famous remark: "I went to communism as one goes to a spring of fresh water.") In Silone's work, towns and people have names like Acquasanta, Acquaviva (literally "living water") or Pietrasecca ("dry stone") indicating their interior life. The cover of his last work was graced with Giotto's fresco of "The Miracle of the Spring," depicting St. Francis of Assisi in prayer while a fellow pilgrim quenches his thirst nearby. But "if the spring is not clear," declares one of Silone's protagonists, "I refuse to drink."[42]

---

[41] "Restare se stesso," in *Il Resto di Carlino*, January 20, 1963; reprinted in *ISRS*, vol. 2, 1264-65. Darina Silone recounts the episode in her *Colloqui*, 88-89.

[42] Rocco De Donatis in *A Handful of Blackberries*, 168.

Italian Antifascist Exiles and the Italian-American Community: Renato Poggioli and Gaetano Salvemini as Case Studies

Charles Killinger

First of all, I know that I am not alone among his students in saying this: Phil Cannistraro was not only a tireless and endlessly tolerant mentor, but a friend. He inspired us, he enriched our lives, he entertained us with his humor, he cajoled us, and he always seemed to know when to apply the whip and when to tease.

I recall a phone conversation in the middle of which Phil dropped a bombshell: Someone else had begun writing the same book I was writing.

"What can *we* do, Phil?"

"Finish your book," he growled, somewhat playfully.

I never did know the veracity of his story, but I always suspected that it was a clever ploy because such counsel seemed to come instinctively to Phil. Jim Burgwyn, Phil's close friend and collaborator, attributed this remarkable talent to a more fundamental trait: "For a man who was entirely contemptuous of moralizing, he was the epitome of authenticity without trying."

Out of respect to Phil, I will keep the tribute brief, except to repeat one friend's response to this conference. Phil would have said: "How nice . . . . It took you long enough."

And to Ernest and Bill and others who have been working for years to make this day possible, a heartfelt thanks.

⸿

This paper evolves from a topic that Phil suggested in Florence years ago: the attempt by Italian antifascist exiles to influence Italian-American communities. In his own inimitable way, Phil led me into the bowels of the Archivio Centrale in Rome where his archivist-friend (and, of course, in Italy one likes to have a friend) pulled down a secret police file that helped to document this dynamic relationship. Holding this file was possible, of course, because of Phil's connections; and the file proved useful because the Fascist regime was acutely aware of antifascist activities and recorded in great detail as much as it could.

The documents in my hands that day in the archive were impressive; Phil needed not say a word. However, in another sense he did, because Phil Cannistraro's research on the experiences of the antifascist exiles and their adversaries in the United States proved enormously influential. Within his larger body of work, he generated groundbreaking studies of Luigi Antonini, Generoso Pope, the Mazzini Society, and Fascist activities in Little Italy, all of which he translated into penetrating, meaningful narrative. In so doing, he literally paved the way for scholars on both sides of the Atlantic, including his students. Few, if any, have mastered as well as he the dynamic of the Fascist era in both Italy and the U. S.—and particularly their interconnections. Phil's methodology proved instructive, in particular his ability to interpret and frame in broad, transatlantic context memoirs, diaries, interviews, and the most detailed archival records. He willingly shared his approach and his insights—even his documents— and he hoped that we could find our way. Those who had the privilege to work with Phil understand not only the power of his work but the generosity of the man.

හ

One approach to understanding this intercultural dynamic is to examine a case study of the successes and failures experienced by two Italian intellectuals, both of whom attempted to mobilize Italian America in a campaign against Fascist Italy. The two men were Gaetano Salvemini of Harvard and Renato Poggioli of Brown. This Salvemini work is not new; however, the work on Poggioli is. It derives from a conference that moved from Smith to Brown, literally following his career, and it is included in a biographical anthology published in 2012. The hope is that by integrating the experiences of these two men more can be learned about both the exiles and about the communities they approached.

In addition to the efforts the two men directed toward Italian America, there exists a transatlantic dimension of their experiences. For neither Salvemini nor Poggioli lived in a vacuum: each had extensive experience in Italy before being forced out, both hoped to return to a post-fascist, democratic Italian republic, and the two both benefited and suffered from their American experiences.

Beyond those generalizations, the two men differed significantly. Salvemini was born in 1873 in Molfetta (Bari Province). He became an antifascist activist in middle age when Fascists murdered Giacomo Matteotti in 1924. The next year, Blackshirt thugs hounded him from his classroom at the University of Florence and beat his lawyer to death. Salvemini eventually escaped from prison guards and made his way to France and ultimately to the United States, where in 1933 he signed his first in a series of one-year teaching contracts.[1]

Renato Poggioli was born in Florence, 34 years after Salvemini. He taught at the University of Florence in 1933 and 1934 and in Polish universities until 1938 when he sought and found a position in the U.S. to escape the growing Nazi menace. Thus for several years in the mid-1930s, Poggioli managed to maintain teaching positions in Europe and at least tacit approval from the semi-official Institutes of Italian Culture in Prague and Warsaw because, unlike Salvemini, he did not at that point engage in overt antifascist activities.[2] By 1940, when he was regularly speaking out in opposition to the regime, the Fascist press was berating and hounding him as was the Italian Embassy through its agents.[3]

Like many refugees from fascist Europe, neither man had a job upon arrival in the U.S., but both managed to find Ivy League positions of indefinite duration. Both were convinced that opposition to the Fascist re-

---

[1] Gaetano Salvemini, *Memorie di un fuoruscito*, Gaetano Arfé, ed (Milan, 1973), 175; Arthur Conant to Salvemini, December 16, 1933; Salvemini to Conant, December 18, 1933; press release, December 20, 1933, Harvard University News Office, 1933, 238; Henry James, Board of Overseers, to Francis W. Hunnewell, Secretary to the Corporation, January 2, 1934; Hunnewell to Henry L. Shattuck, Treasurer, Harvard College, January 3, 1934; Clarence Henry Haring, Chairman, Department of History, to Salvemini, January 19, 1934; Ruth Draper to President and Fellows of Harvard College, May 1, 1939, *James B. Conant Papers*, Harvard University Archives, Cambridge, MA.

[2] "Renato Poggioli," *Harvard University Gazette* 60 (1964); Poggioli, letter to Neilson, April 26, 1944, Smith College Archives (SCA), Faculty Collection (FC), box 42, "Poggioli." Poggioli provided the following account of his previous career to Smith College: "Lectura Dantis and Contemporary Italian Literature, Professor of the summer courses at the University, Florence 1933; Russian Language and Literature, Professor at the University, Florence 1933-34; Secretary, Istituto di Cultura Italiana, Prague 1934-35; Italian Language and Literature, Lecturer at the University, Wilno, Poland, 1935-37; Warsaw 1937-38; Modern Italian Poetry, Istituto di Cultura Italiana, Warsaw, 1937-38," SCA, FC, box 42, "Poggioli Visiting Lecturer Folder;" See also L. Pertile, M. Riva, and R. Ludovico, eds. *Renato Poggioli, An Intellectual Biography* (Florence: 2012).

[3] Killinger, "Renato Poggioli and Antifascism in the United States" in *Renato Poggioli, An Intellectual Biography*.

gime—especially Italian-American opposition—could influence U.S. policy and thus the future of Italy. For that reason, the two professors in 1939 joined in founding the antifascist Mazzini Society.[4]

Salvemini's greatest efforts were in Boston and New York City, Poggioli's in Providence. In each place, the Fascist regime used consular officials and *agents provocateurs* to spy on them and disrupt their activities. It is this experience—particularly as it reflects their efforts to make inroads among Italian-Americans—on which this paper will focus. What factors most influenced their respective campaigns?

THEIR VALUES

Of primary importance were their values. Among the many threads that united Poggioli and Salvemini in their antifascist campaigns was a commitment to values derived from the Enlightenment, most basically freedom. Poggioli's Harvard colleague Adam Ulam detected a strain of Jacobinism in his thought: "As he adhered to the Continental radical tradition, authority of all kinds was suspect in Poggioli's mind."[5] But this skilled translator and scholar of comparative literature preferred to express his opposition to Fascism in broad, cultural terms.[6] One scholar believes that Poggioli's antifascism developed from *"cultura e civiltà, più che per ragioni ideologiche ."*[7]

Poggioli's own accounts seem to confirm the view that his motivation was fundamentally cultural. For example, in 1940, Poggioli wrote: *"Ho lasciato l'Italia e son venuto in America al solo scopo di poter finalmente vivere*

---

[4] In September 1939, Salvemini joined Roberto Bolaffio, Lionello Venturi, Renato Poggioli, and Michele Cantarella at the Cantarella home on the Smith College campus in Northampton, Massachusetts to create the new antifascist organization. They agreed to mount a new campaign to mobilize the American public and American policy makers against totalitarianism, monarchism and clericalism, with a particular eye toward the post-war reconstruction of a democratic Italy. "Relazione della prima seduta della Mazzini Society," signed by Poggioli and Venturi, n.d., Istituto Storico della Resistenza in Toscano (ISRT), *Mazzini Society (MS)*, f. 1, sf. 2. See also Killinger, *Salvemini*, 281-99.

[5] Adam B. Ulam, *Understanding the Cold War: A Historian's Personal Reflections* (Charlottesville, 2000), 80. See also Dante Della Terza, *Da Vienna a Baltimora: La Diaspora degli intellettuali europei negli stati uniti d'America* (Rome, 1987).

[6] Laurent Béghin, "Uno Slavista Comparatista sotto il Fascismo: Gli Anni di Formazione di Renato Poggioli (1928-1938)," *Archivio Russo-Italiano* 4 (Salerno, 2005), 424.

[7] Giuseppe Ghini, "Renato Poggioli (1907-1963)." 8 June 2007 <http://www.uniurb.it/lingue/docenti/ghini/biobibliografia> (last update September 21, 2005), 1.

in un regime di liberta e democrazia."[8] And again, in 1943: "A dishonored and submissive Italy will mean a world less beautiful and less civil. The nation of Dante and Michelangelo, of Columbus and Leonardo, of Bruno and Galileo, of Mazzini and Garibaldi still has and always will have a great mission to fulfill for Europe and the human race."[9]

In contrast, Salvemini was the consummate pragmatist, ever focused on a specific program of political and economic reform. He always considered himself a non-Marxist socialist, and thus his criticisms were stated with greater social emphasis than those of Poggioli. Throughout the *ventennio*, Salvemini hammered away point-by-point at the Fascist regime's claims of economic progress and at their oft-repeated themes of propaganda.[10] For example, he used sources that he had collected since leaving Italy in 1925 to demonstrate that Fascist policies had undermined the eight-hour day, had driven down real wages, and had achieved what they called "social peace," not by economic planning but by the coercion of a police state.[11]

Their mutual commitments to Enlightenment-based values of political freedom led both Poggioli and Salvemini to oppose not only Fascism, but also communism, an ideology both found ill-suited to Italian culture.[12] The result was to alienate a potential ally in Italian-American communists, which was only a first step in limiting their options. Both men took strong stands against communist membership in the Mazzini Society and led vocal campaigns in their respective communities. Salvemini's pragmatism led him to focus on Marxist practices rather than ideology, condemning Stalinism as dictatorship of the left.[13] And as the war turned

[8] Copy of Renato Poggioli, letter to Direttore dell'*Eco del Rhode Island*, February 9, 1940, Archivio Centrale dello Stato (Rome) (ACS), *Ministero del'Interno* (MI), Direzione Generale Pubblica Sicurezza (DGPS), (1940) Cat. A1, b. 67, f. "Poggioli."

[9] Poggioli, draft of speech ("Appello agl'italiani d'America"), n.d. (June 1943?), Fondo Poggioli (Rome) *(FP)*.

[10] See, for example, Salvemini, *Under the Axe of Fascism* (New York, 1936).

[11] Ibid., 144-366.

[12] Poggioli, letter to Salvemini, October 1, 1939, ISRT, *MS*, f. 2, sf. 2; Alessandra Baldini and Paolo Palma, *Gli antifascisti italiani in America (1942-1944): La "Legione" nel carteggio di Pacciardi con Borgese, Salvemini, Sforza e Sturzo* (Florence, 1990).

[13] Salvemini, "Dittatura e democrazia," *Scritti Vari (1900-1957),* 453-459; "Il mito dell'uomo-Dio," *Giustizia e Libertà* (Paris), July 20, 1934; Gaetano Salvemini Scrapbooks, Houghton Library, Harvard University; "La difesa della cultura," *Scritti Vari,* 668-670.

toward Allied victory, both opposed a PCI government in post-fascist Italy.[14]

Their commitment to secular, democratic values additionally led both adamantly to oppose the monarchy and the Catholic Church. Opposition to the Savoy dynasty merely put them at odds with the Churchill government, but anticlericalism created yet another breach with the Italian-American community.[15]

THEIR LIMITATIONS

If opposition both to communist and Catholic leadership narrowed their options, both men faced other limitations. As would-be community organizers, neither had real-world experience. Salvemini, in particular, found distasteful the bargaining and manipulation that are often necessary in unifying a campaign. In 1919 Ettore Rota had called Salvemini "the anti-Machiavelli of contemporary society." A half-century later, Ascoli labeled him "the greatest enemy of politics of all the men I have ever known."[16]

Nor was Poggioli comfortable with organizational politics. Continuing internal disputes within the Providence chapter of the Mazzini Society, including evictions and allegations that one member was collaborating with Fascists, led Poggioli to the brink of resignation.[17]

Salvemini's disdain for those who engaged in such "corrupt bargains" was palpable. It further alienated him from other groups in the New York area that could have become assets, most notably the unions and the socialist party and their Italian American leaders who generally were critics of the Fascist regime. These men, such as Luigi Antonini of the ILGWU,

---

[14] Randolfo Pacciardi, letters to Poggioli, November 28, 1942, February 26, March 16, and April 22, 1943, *FP*. Students of Pacciardi will want to see his lengthy political testament ("io resto fedele alla scuola repubblicana . . . perchè è un scuola socialista italiana.") Pacciardi, letter to Poggioli, April 22, 1943, *FP*.

[15] Salvemini, *The Origins of Fascism in Italy* (New York, 1973), 137-49; Salvemini and George LaPiana, *What to Do with Italy* (New York, 1943), 32-49.

[16] Ettore Rota, "Una pagina di storia contemporanea: Gaetano Salvemini," *Nuova Rivista Storica*, III (May-August 1919), 322; Max Ascoli, "Salvemini negli Stati Uniti," *La Voce Repubblicana*, December 20-21, 1967, 16-24; Gian Giacomo Migone, *Problemi di storia nei rapporti tra l'Italia e Stati Uniti* (Turin, 1971) 95, 154; Antonio Donno, "Gli stati uniti vista da Salvemini" in Gaetano Cingari, ed., *Gaetano Salvemini tra politica e storia* (Bari, 1986), 406-409.

[17] Tarchiani, letters to Poggioli, 24 August, 1 and 25 September 1942, *FP*.

had fully assimilated and in the process had learned to play "hardball" in the style of American politics—a style antithetical to the professors.[18]

And if their potential allies were street-wise, their pro-fascist adversaries were even more so—and better funded. The publisher Generoso Pope was similarly assimilated, an even more powerful presence in Little Italy than Antonini, and connected to FDR's machine as head of the Italian section of the Democratic Party.[19] The result was that both Poggioli and Salvemini, in their respective communities, worked at a decided disadvantage as they attempted to convert Italian-Americans to their cause.[20]

Another factor that identified the two men was the transatlantic aspect of their experiences, and this, too, made their tasks difficult. Both considered themselves Italians—in spite of American citizenship—and both hoped to return to their birth country. Both men were exiles, labeled *"fuorusciti"* by the Fascists, and were not in any sense immigrants. Most obviously, they had not undergone any process of assimilation or acculturation outside the halls of academe. In spite of American citizenship and Poggioli's service in the U.S. Army, the two men were *in* the U.S. but not *of* the U.S., and this very fact further inhibited their efforts.[21]

---

[18] Cannistraro, "Antonini," 21-40; Salvemini to Alberto Tarchiani, November 4, 1932, May 7 and June 5, 1933, *Alberto Tarchiani Papers, Archivio Giustizia e Libertà (AGL)*, ISRT; Vanni B. Montana, *Amarostico, Testimonianze euro-americane* (Livorno 1975),173-175; Ascoli to Salvemini, March 10, 1941, *Max Ascoli Papers*, "Salvemini file," Manuscript Collections, Boston University; Salvemini to Tarchiani, February 26, 1941 and Tarchiani to Salvemini, March 1, 1941, *Tarchiani Papers*; Roberto Bolaffio to Salvemini, April 18, 1941, *AGL*, ISRT "Salvemini."

[19] Cannistraro, "Generoso Pope and the Rise of Italian American Politics, 1925-1936" in Lydio F. Tomasi, ed., *Italian Americans, New Perspectives in Italian Immigration & Ethnicity* (Staten Island, 1985), 264-288; John P. Diggins, *Mussolini and Fascism, The View from America* (Princeton, 1972), 84-86; Salvemini, *Italian Fascist Activities in the United States*, P. V. Cannistraro, ed. (Staten Island, 1977), 9.

[20] Cannistraro, "Per una storia dei fasci negli stati uniti, 1921-1929," *Storia Contemporanea*, 26.1 (December 1995), 1089-1144.

[21] Poggioli had filed his "intention to become a citizen" upon his arrival in the U.S. Poggioli, letter, n.d. (late 1943?), *FP*. He wrote that he filed his formal application for citizenship at least twice while on active duty, only to be rejected, at which point he requested a discharge in order to join the Italian forces fighting alongside the Allies, especially if he could contribute to the liberation of Florence. According to Poggioli, the denial of citizenship was based on an FBI report related to his Mazzini Society activities, his support for a Free Italy movement, and his public statements about foreign policy. From September 1943 through September 1945, Poggioli served in the U.S. army; in 1950, after a struggle, he finally became a U.S. citizen. "Renato Poggioli," *Harvard University Gazette* 60

THE COMMUNITIES

In order to fully understand their difficulties, it is also essential to look inside the Italian-American communities. On his first speaking tour of the U. S. in 1927, Salvemini found Italian-Americans receptive to his antifascist message. Only later did he realize that those audiences were not typical and only later did he understand why they were susceptible to Fascist propaganda.[22] As immigrants, discrimination and vilification had created a new sense of ethnic identity, which, in turn, had magnified their pride in their native country. Cannistraro has suggested that "fascist propaganda was more successful among Italian Americans in the United States than it was . . . in Italy."[23] The result was that they were especially receptive to the hyper-nationalist propaganda generated by the regime, perpetuated by the embassy, and passed along uncritically by Pope and other publishers. Reflecting on this issue in 1940, Salvemini wrote:

> [Italian immigrants] had never felt themselves to be Italians as long as they had been living in the old country. . . . National consciousness awoke in them when they came in touch (which often meant to blows) with groups of different national origins in America. Italy now seemed to them no longer a land from which they had been forced to leave. . . .[24]

And finally, their criticisms of the Fascist regime often made Poggioli and Salvemini appear to be anti-Italian. By the mid-1930s—especially after the Ethiopian War—Salvemini had become acutely aware of this. He knew that a heightened sense of *Italianità* among immigrants had led

---

(1964); Poggioli, letter to William Allan Neilson, April 26, 1944, SCA, FC, box 42, "Poggioli."

[22] Salvemini, *Memorie*, 61-62; Enzo Tagliacozzo, "Nota biografica" in Eugenio Garin et al, *Gaetano Salvemini* (Bari, 1959), 257-58; Diggins, *Mussolini and Fascism*, 148; Cannistraro, Introduction to Salvemini, *Italian Fascist Activities*, xv; Salvemini, *Memorie*, 63; Charles Killinger interview with Michele and Hélène Cantarella, Leeds, Massachusetts, 1979; Salvemini to Oswald Villard, January 16, 1927, Houghton Library, Harvard University; Copy of telegram, Italian Ambassador (Washington) to Ministro degli Affari Esteri (MAE), January 12, 1927, MI, DGPS, *Casellario politico centrale* (CPC), ACS, "Salvemini" file; *Christian Science Monitor*, January 15, 1927. In "Fascism and Italian Americans," 134, Cannistraro suggested that "fascist propaganda was more successful among Italian Americans in the United States than it was . . . in Italy." See also Killinger, *Salvemini*, 210-228.

[23] Cannistraro, "Fascism and Italian Americans," 134.

[24] Salvemini, *Italian Fascist Activities*, 4.

them to confuse Fascism with Italy, so that his attacks were always at risk of being misinterpreted.

Their Dilemmas

In addition to these fundamental problems, the two scholars were forced almost constantly to adjust tactics in the face of rapidly escalating conditions. First Ascoli converted the Mazzini Society that they had founded to an American lobbying group, which Antonini then took over.[25] Italy's invasion of France in June 1940 brought an influx of antifascist exiles and new campaigns—for example, Randolfo Pacciardi's Free Italy movement, modeled after De Gaulle's Free France.[26] Pacciardi then advocated admitting communists—alongside of whom he had fought in the Spanish Civil War—to the Mazzini Society. The Pearl Harbor attack and the U.S. declaration of war on Italy made non-citizen Italian residents Enemy Aliens. And Churchill's influence in supporting the House of Savoy in the postwar settlement undercut their republican campaign.[27] This chain of events overwhelmed the activist efforts of the two professors and doomed them largely to the position of passive observers and critics.

Their Successes

In the final analysis, what do we make of the political achievements of these two accomplished scholars? If evaluated simply on the basis of their successes in mobilizing grass-roots opposition to the Fascist regime in their respective Little Italies, both Poggioli and Salvemini failed. Philosophically, one can accept that failure because they never really had a chance. Twenty years of Fascist propaganda and a leadership class including many pro-Fascist *prominenti* was simply too much for a small cadre of intellectuals to overcome.

However, it is also true that Salvemini and Poggioli put forward in the mainstream American press and in U. S. diplomatic channels a strong

---

[25] Cannistraro, "Antonini"; Killinger, *Salvemini*, 281-99.

[26] MI (Rome) to CPC, April 26, 1941; undated memo, "Italian Emergency Rescue Committee," CPC "Salvemini" file; Tarchiani to Giorgio LaPiana, September 11, 1940, *Giorgio LaPiana Papers*, Andover-Harvard Theological Library, Cambridge, MA; Aldo Garosci, *Storia die fuorusciti* (Bari, 1953), 208; Max Salvadori, *Resistenza ed azione* (Bari, 1961), 189-191.

[27] Killinger, *Salvemini*, 286-92; Maddalena Tirabassi, "Enemy Aliens or Loyal Americans? The Mazzini Society and the Italian-American Communities," *Atti del Settimo Convegno Nazionale: Italy and Italians in America*. Alfredo Rizzardi, ed. *Rivista di Studi Anglo-Americani* 3 (1984-85): 399-425.

case for a secular democratic republic and provided the State Department with a clear rationale for opposing the more conservative agenda of the Churchill government. In 1943, as the U.S. forces fought their way north through the peninsula, Salvemini was in regular contact with the U. S. forces, and he recommended that the U.S. rely on his trusted friends, most connected with the Partito d'Azione.[28] He also was in contact with Piero Calamandrei, who represented the Pd'A at the constituent assembly that drafted the republican constitution.[29] The degree to which their influence contributed substantially to the constitution of the Italian Republic is questionable, but in its outlines, the constitution conformed to their most fundamental values.

THEIR RETURN TO ITALY

And, finally, their opposition to Stalinism shaped their respective postwar lives. With the demise of the Partito d'Azione, Salvemini's hopes for a *terza forza* of the democratic left were crushed. He spent his final years criticizing both the DC and the PCI, while writing in *Il Mondo, Il Ponte, Critica Sociale,* and other Italian journals in support of such causes as electoral reform, European federation, and civil liberties.[30] In 1957 at age 83, Salvemini died among friends at an idyllic villa in Capo di Sorrento.

Poggioli suffered more directly from his American political activities. This brilliant scholar struggled mightily to publish his works, largely as a result of his previous anti-Communism and his interest in Stalinist dissident writers. His prospects of publishing in postwar Italy were dashed when the PCI intervened with the board of Einaudi to block the publication of two of Poggioli's books: *Il fiore del verso russo,* a compilation of Russian writers, some of them dissidents, and his *La teoria dell'arte d'avanguardia.*[31] In 1963, while teaching at Berkeley, Poggioli died tragically in an auto accident, prematurely ending a promising academic career.

---

[28] Killinger, "An Italian in America, an American in Italy: Unpublished Letters from Gaetano Salvemini to Stephen Tanner (July-October 1944)," *The Italian American Review* 6. 2 (Autumn/Winter 1998).

[29] Tanner to GS, September 22, 1944, Tanner Letters (personal possession of the author); GS to Piero Calamandrei, October 13, 1944; Gaetano Salvemini, *Lettere dall'America 1944/1946,* Alberto Merola, ed. (Bari, 1967), 25.

[30] Killinger, *Salvemini,* 316-27.

[31] This exchange, largely between Poggioli and Cesare Pavese, is documented in Pertile, L. M. Riva, and R. Ludovico, eds. *Renato Poggioli, An Intellectual Biography.*

REFERENCES

Baldini, Alessandra and Paolo Palma. *Gli antifascisti italiani in America (1942-1944): La "Legione" nel carteggio di Pacciardi con Borgese, Salvemini, Sforza e Sturzo*. Florence, 1990.

Bėghin, Laurent. "Uno slavista comparatista sotto il fascismo: Gli anni di formazione di Renato Poggioli (1928-1938)." *Archivio Russo-Italiano* IV (Salerno, 2005), 395-446.

Cingari, Gaetano ed. *Gaetano Salvemini tra politica e storia*. Bari, 1986.

Cannistraro, Philip V. *Blackshirts in Little Italy: Italian Americans and Fascism, 1921-1929*. West Lafayette, IN, 1999.

_____. "Luigi Antonini and the Italian Anti-Fascist Movement in the United States, 1940-1943." *Journal of American Ethnic History* 1 (Fall 1985): 21-40.

_____. "Per una storia dei fasci negli Stati Uniti, 1921-1929." *Storia Contemporanea* 26. 1 (December 1995): 1061-1144.

_____. "Fascism and Italian Americans in Detroit, 1933-35," *International Migration Review* 9.1 (1975): 29-40.

_____. "Generoso Pope and the Rise of Italian American Politics, 1925-1936." In *Italian Americans, New Perspectives in Italian Immigration & Ethnicity*. Edited by Lydio Tomasi, 264-288. Staten Island, 1985.

Della Terza, Dante. *Da Vienna a Baltimora: La diaspora degli intellecttuali europi negli Stati Uniti d'America*. Rome, 1987.

Diggins, John P. *Mussolini and Fascism, The View from America*. Princeton, 1972.

Garosci, Aldo. *Storia dei fuorusciti*. Bari, 1953.

Ghini, Giuseppe. "Renato Poggioli (1907-1963)." June 8, 2007. <http://www.uniurb.it/lingue/docenti/ghini/biobibliografia> (last update 21 September 2005), 1.

Killinger, Charles. "An Italian in America, an American in Italy: Unpublished Letters from Gaetano Salvemini to Stephen Tanner (July-October 1944)." *The Italian American Review* 6.2 (Autumn/Winter 1998): 98-122.

_____. *Gaetano Salvemini, A Biography*. Westport CT, 2002.

Migone, Gian Giacomo. *Problemi di storia nei rapporti tra l'Italia e Stati Uniti*. Turin, 1971.

Pertile, L., M. Riva, and R. Ludovico, eds. *Renato Poggioli, An Intellectual Biography*. Florence, 2012.

"Renato Poggioli." *Harvard University Gazette* 60 (1964).

Salvadori, Max. *Resistenza ed azione*. Bari, 1961.

Salvemini, Gaetano. *Italian Fascist Activities in the United States*. P. V. Cannistraro, ed. Staten Island, 1977.

_____. *Memorie di un fuorusciti*. Gaetano Arfé, ed. Milan, 1973.

_____. *Movimento socialista e questione meridionale*, Gaetano Arfe, ed. Milan, 1961.

_____. *The Origins of Fascism in Italy*. New York, 1973.

_____. *Scritti Vari (1900-1957)*. Milan, 1978.

_____. *Under the Axe of Fascism*. New York, 1936.

_____ and George LaPiana. *What to Do with Italy*. New York, 1943.

Tirabassi, Maddalena. "Enemy Aliens or Loyal Americans? The Mazzini Society and the Italian-American Communities." *Atti del Settimo Convegno Nazionale: Italy and Italians in America*.

Alfredo Rizzardi, ed. *Rivista di Studi Anglo-Americani* 3 (1984-85): 399-425.

Tomasi, Lydio ed. *Italian Americans, New Perspectives in Italian Immigration & Ethnicity*. Staten Island, 1985.

Ulam, Adam B. *Understanding the Cold War: A Historian's Personal Reflections*. Charlottesville, 2000.

New York City's Italian Americans and the Great Depression: The Response of a Community in Distress

Gerald Meyer

For a time [the residents of the Little Italies'] dual identities as proletarians and as Italians were congruent sources of solidarity.

—Rudolph Vecoli.

Introduction

During the Great Depression, New York City's Italian Americans endured the greatest hardships of any of the city's larger European-derived communities. The deteriorated state of the Italian American community—relative to other European-derived nationalities—is evidenced by its members' concentration in substandard housing, significantly higher rates of lower-income employment, and greatly heightened levels of unemployment and dependence on Home Relief.

New York City's Italians Americans were the most proletarianized of all the European nationality groups. Their numbers in the middle class were small and still less in the professional/managerial strata. Fourteen percent of the city's white population as a whole received some sort of public assistance; more than one in five Italian Americans received public assistance—a figure 50 percent higher than the city's overall average (Wenger 1996, 17). They represented the greatest percentage of workers engaged in Work Projects Administration undertakings of any European-derived group (Federal Writers' Project 1938, 60). (Eligibility for Home Relief was a prerequisite for being hired for WPA jobs.)

The prevailing narrative of the Italian American experience has neither acknowledged adequately the severity of socio-economic conditions for Italian Americans in New York City (and by extension elsewhere in the United States) nor integrated the profound social and political consequences engendered by this calamity. Since the publication in 1938 of the Federal Writers' Project-sponsored *The Italians of New York* there has been no book-length historical study devoted to the experience of New York

City's Italian Americans during the long decade from the New York Stock Market Crash, of October 29, 1929, to the United States entry into World War II, on December 7, 1941. *The Italians of New York* boldly asserted, "First-generation Italian immigrants performed, by and large, the meanest tasks in return for meager wages and systematic discriminatory practices" (Federal Writers' Project 1938, 51). Despite its populist, documentary approach, which elsewhere has been described as "social democratic," the organizing idea of this commercially successful survey was assimilationist. Its conclusion, matter-of-factly (even approvingly), predicted that eventually, "Most of New York's schools' . . . 300 thousand 'Italian' children . . . will no longer be bilingual . . . and they will disappear into that countless mass of native Americans whose origin it is as difficult to establish as it is to trace the streams whose waters have flowed into the ocean" (Federal Writers' Project 1938, 224-225; Mangione 1972; Dittman 1999, np).

This paper posits that during this dynamic decade a different—and better—outcome for New York City's Italian Americans was possible. Embedded in the disadvantages besetting the city's Italian Americans lay positive potential. The massive unemployment and dependence on Home Relief and WPA powerfully connected this community to the New Deal and their concentration in an archipelago of Little Italies gave them political bases for their participation in America's version of the Popular Front. These communities also were sites which inspired and verified cultural-pluralist assumptions associated with New Deal politics and thought, and countered the forces of Americanization. The progressive awakening of New York's Italian American community was most fully realized in Italian Harlem, which will be discussed here in some detail.

Underlying each of the sections of this essay—"Demographics," "Income/Remuneration," "Occupations/Unemployment," "Little Italies," "Emergence of a Distinctive Culture," "Politics," and "Italian Harlem"— are two assumptions: New York City's Italian Americans (and by extension to Italian Americans living elsewhere under similar conditions) constituted a cultural minority; and this culture did not represent an obstacle to this community's adoption of a progressive politics and could, in fact, provide a basis for Left politics.

DEMOGRAPHICS

On the eve of the Great Depression, Italian Americans were the second largest nationality group in New York City. The 1930 United States Census, which was the first to collect data on the number of first- and second-generation Americans (Shedd 1934, "Foreword," 3, 14), counted 1,070,355 first- and second-generation Italian American New Yorkers. As defined by the 1930 Census, the rubric "Italian Americans" included only the first- (Italian-born) and second-generation (that is, American-born with at least one parent born in Italy). Third-generation Italian Americans, that is, those who had at least one second-generation Italian American parent, were classified under the rubric "native white of native parentage." In 1930, first- and second-generation Italians comprised roughly 85 percent of the total Italian American population in the United States (Alba 1985, 47). Had they been included, third-generation Italian Americans (American-born with at least one Italian-born parent), who constituted the vast majority of the remaining Italian Americans, would have increased these numbers by approximately 10 percent. In 1930, the percentage of Italian Americans who were fourth generation was miniscule.

The Census Bureau's exclusion of third-generation Italian Americans as full-fledged members of the Italian American communities unreasonably reduced the "official" Italian population. In the late 1930s, Covello created a remarkably well conceived questionnaire that he had administered to three cohorts of East Harlem high-school boys (second-generation Italian Americans, third-generation Italian Americans, and "others") that verified his supposition that "outward and superficial aspects of Americanization" obscured the retention of Southern Italian family mores in the life patterns of second- and third-generation Italian Americans (Covello 1967, 360-370, 372-381, 349). The responses to Covello's questionnaire substantiated his assertion, "As concerns Italians in a community like East Harlem, . . . all adjustments, all accommodations are made in terms of an Italian environment" (Covello 1945, 6).

The 1940 Census did not seek to identify second-generation Italian Americans. Consequently the only means of estimating the number of second-generation Italian Americans from that date is to establish the percentage of first-generation Italian Americans as a percentage of all the foreign-born in any district and then use that ratio to extract the percentage of second-generation Italian Americans (Bayor 1988, 180). These figures are estimates acceptable for generalizations. Simply tracking the number of first-generation (foreign-born) Italians is tricky, but it can yield some validity. In this essay, when I say that the number of Italians increased/decreased, this means that the number of first-generation Italians had increased. I am leaving the task of extrapolating from these figures' additional numbers of second and third-generation to future studies. In other words, the statistics cited for "Italians" in 1940 are a rough extrapolation from the only statistics we have, that is, the number of foreign-born Italian Americans. These are useful statistics that accurately indicate tendencies and trends, but they are not precise. Covello and others estimated the number of first- , second- , and third-generation Italian Americans in New York City in 1940 at approximately 1,500,000. While this figure is a high estimate, the slow movement of Italian Americans from the city (and for that matter out of their traditional sites of settlement within the city) during the Depression, and the very large numbers of second-generation Italian Americans entering the "family building" stage during this decade suggest that Covello's calculation is reasonably accurate (Covello 1945, 1).

Throughout this paper, information is organized and presented from the City's 310 Health Areas, statistical units, each of which included roughly 25,000 people living under similar social and economic conditions, and twenty Health Center Districts, which in 1940 encompassed from 130,000 to 438,000 residents; for example, they included ten Health Areas in the Lower West Side in Manhattan, and seven in Pelham Bay in the Bronx.

New York City's Italian Americans in 1930 constituted roughly one-fourth of the first- and second-generation Italian American population in the United States.[1] Until 1954, when it ceased functioning as an entry station for immigrants, 96 percent of those Italians who immigrated to the United States first landed at Ellis Island (Cannistraro 1999, 5). New York City remains the great metropolis of the Italian American experience; in 2006, 8 percent of its population (including those indicating multiple identities) self-identified as Italian American (Milione and Gambino 2009, 24). Consequently, at least until their dispersal during World War II and its aftermath, what can be discerned from a study of New York City's Italian American communities substantially applies to other cities, small and

---

[1] The 1930 Census counted 4,546,788 first- and second-generation Italians in the United States (Shedd 1934, 14). New York City's largest group, the Jews, comprised 40 percent of the Jewish population in the United States (Wenger 1996, 6, 8). In 1930, Italians were the largest foreign-born group in the United States (Tomasi 1975, 15).

large, especially in the Northeast and Midwest industrial belts, where the largest numbers of Italian Americans settled.[2]

INCOME/REMUNERATION

Italian Americans, on average, were the poorest of all of New York City's European-derived groups. The 1930 U.S. Census collected data on the median monthly housing costs for households of first-generation immigrants of twenty-nine ethnic groups in New York City. Aside from two small immigrant communities (Portuguese and Czech Americans), the Census showed that the median rent for Italian Americans—$32.59—was the lowest for all these groups.[3]

With only few exceptions, New York City's Little Italies were low-rent, largely tenement districts such as East Harlem and Williamsburg, and areas of relatively recent development located near the termini of recently constructed subway lines, such as Belmont in the Bronx, and Bensonhurst in Brooklyn (Shedd 1934, 3). In Manhattan, there were very few Italian Americans in the three Health Center District with above median monthly rent ($38): the Upper West Side ($52), the Upper East Side ($47), and Washington Heights-Inwood ($46). Central Harlem, which had slightly below median rents, housed only handfuls of Italians. "Italians" were concentrated in the three Health Center Districts with below the $38 median monthly rent—the Lower West Side ($33), which included Greenwich Village and part of the Mulberry Street Little Italy; East Harlem ($25), which, embraced Italian Harlem and the ethnically mixed areas along its borders; and the heavily Jewish Lower East Side ($23), which included part of the Mulberry Street and the South Village Little Italies (Health Center 1944, 6, 68-103).

Within each of the heavily Italian American Health Center Districts, the predominantly Italian American Health Areas had the lowest or near-lowest rents. In the Lower West Side Health Center District, the three

---

[2] The concentration of Italian Americans within New York City was part of a larger concentration. In 1930 almost 73 percent of the Italian Americans lived in six contiguous northeast states—New York, New Jersey, Massachusetts, Pennsylvania, Connecticut, and Rhode Island. According to the 1990 Census, over one half (56 percent) of all Italian Americans continued to live in those six states (Covello 1934, 119; Starr 2000, 504).

[3] The immigrant groups paying the highest median monthly rents derived from: English-speaking Canada, $65.34; Northern Ireland, $59.21; the Netherlands, $55.10; Scotland, $54.10; Rumania, $52.33; Russia, $52.39. The vast majority of New York City residents from Russia, Austria-Hungary, and Rumania were Jewish (*Bureau of the Census* 1930, 171).

Health Areas that had the lowest rents ($21 to $22), Italian Americans predominated. In the Lower East Side, Italian Americans shared the misery of living in the absolutely worst housing, which in five Health Areas rented for $19 per month. In East Harlem's ten Health Areas, Italians predominated in seven, four of which had the lowest median monthly rents ($20-$24) (Health Center 1944, p 70-75, 80-83, 86-89). These patterns repeated themselves in New York City's four other boroughs. In Brooklyn, the Williamsburg Health Center District, directly across the East River from the Lower East Side Health Center District, mirrored its social characteristics: the Italians shared low-rent districts with poor Jews, and had a median rent ($24) that was one dollar higher. Italian Americans predominated in the low-rent Health Center Districts of Red Hook ($25), Bushwick ($26), and Fort Greene ($31). Within these low-rent Health Center Districts, they predominated in the lowest rent Health Areas. The Italian American population in the Bronx repeated this general pattern. In Queens, the Italian American population was less clustered, so generalizations require much more refined statistical analyses. However, there were a few significant and thought-provoking variations. In the two heaviest Italian American Health Areas (6.10, 6.20) in the Pelham Bay Health Center District, in the northeast Bronx, they had median rents ($42 and $46) that were near the Health Center District's median ($43). These Health Areas formed the nucleus for a predominantly Italian American middle-class community, which had characteristics of American suburbia (one- and two-family homes) and of the Little Italies (ethnic stores) (Health Center 1944, p 112-126, 138-140, 148-150, 156-158, 164-166).

Though much less than in earlier years, a large part of the Italian immigrants' income was generated by women and children working at home doing piece work (finishing garments, making artificial flowers, shelling nuts) as well as "taking in" boarders. Italian men worked in low-paying, often seasonal, jobs (Guglielmo 2010, 58-59, 62, 68-72, 80, 91-92; Gabaccia 1988, 103, 115, 134). So in the absence of specific information, household income of Italian Americans at that time in New York City can best be correlated with median monthly rents, data collected to serve the purposes of the Health Areas. However, this metric tends to underestimate the incomes of Italian American households. In 1930, when the median size of a foreign-born headed household was 3.76, the city's Italian American households averaged 4.47 persons, which was the highest of the twenty-eight ethnic groups with a population of fifty thousand or more. Consequently, Italian American households included more wage earners than the other European groups. Italian American consumption patterns also differed widely from other European-derived nationality groups. Compared with other nationalities, Italian Americans spent less on housing and more of their meager incomes on food and ceremonial occasions (holidays, rites of passage, and Sunday dinners). Moreover, the percentage of income Italian American families allocated to savings (often to purchase a home or to start up a business) was also relatively high. During the Depression, low-income families moved frequently, in search of the cheapest quarters; at times, they formed "partner households," where more than one family shared the same apartment. In an effort to reduce further their housing costs, families frequently rented to "roomers" (Gabaccia 2000, 103).

Occupations/Unemployment

On July 2, 1932 in Chicago during his acceptance speech before an ecstatic throng assembled at the Democratic Party's nominating convention, Roosevelt called the Great Depression "these unprecedented and unusual times." In New York City this meant one-third of men and women in 1935, who had been employed in 1930, had lost their jobs. This represented a rate of unemployment significantly exceeding the national average of 25 percent (Taylor 2009, 9). The Depression exposed Italian Americans to a disproportionate share of its most dreaded consequence—joblessness. From 1880 to 1920, the great mass of Italians who arrived in the United States were *contadini*, from Italy's *Mezzogiorno*. An early historian of the Italian American experience explained, "[The Southern Italian immigrants] formed an army of unskilled workers with few technicians and almost no professionals among them" (Tomasi 1975, 24). Italian American men were heavily concentrated in the lowest-paying occupations, such as laborers; large numbers were traditional craftsmen (such as, stone cutters, barbers, tailors, bakers, and musicians); all of whom incurred higher-than-average rates of unemployment. As late as 1940 musicians, an occupation disproportionately comprised of Italian American males, had an unemployment rate of 27 percent (D'Alesandre 1935, 5, 15). The economic collapse caused nearly one-half of all manufacturing workers, another category swelled by Italian American men, to lose their jobs. Italian American women comprised 51 percent of the women workers in the garment industry, which was especially hard hit because, unlike food and shelter, most clothing purchases could be deferred. (The other female garment workers were 32 percent Jewish, 5 percent African-American, 2.5 percent Latin American—mostly Puerto Rican) (Guglielmo 2010, 242, 250).

The relative absence of Italian Americans from those sectors of the economy less affected by the Great Depression complete this negative profile. Italian Americans were under-represented in the private-sector, white-collar occupations. Fewer than 2 percent of Italian Americans in New York worked in professional or managerial occupations; this sector, which comprised 13 percent of the city's workforce, experienced only a 5 percent rate of unemployment (Greenberg 1991, 65-66). In the civil service, another area where Italian Americans were relatively few, only one percent of public-service workers subsisted on Home Relief allowances (Bayor 1998, 162). The seasonal nature of much of Italian American men's employment (as laborers and unskilled and skilled workers in construction) resulted in unusually high rates of irregular employment (Cohen 1993, 43-44). In short, even during prosperous times, Italian New Yorkers experienced low rates of remuneration interspersed with periodic unemployment.

Another factor burdened the Italian American workforce. The occupations hardest hit by the Depression fell into the same low-wage sectors of the economy that tended to recover at the slowest pace. As late as 1940, while war preparation caused unemployment to significantly decline nationally, in New York City it remained stubbornly high at an average rate of 18.3. In Italian Harlem, 34.6 percent, nearly double the city-wide average of its working population, remained unemployed (Shedd 1934, 5; Health Center 1944, 86-89).[4] In New York's Little Italies, the Great Depression arrived early and stayed late.

LITTLE ITALIES

The Little Italies represented the greatest accomplishment of the Italian immigrants and their children in the United States. Covello noted that by 1940 a large majority of New York's Italian Americans clustered in thirty-nine Little Italies (Covello 1945, 10). Several of these Little Italies, such as Mulberry Street and the South [Greenwich] Village, were contiguous; very few, and most peculiarly, East New York's Little Italy, were

---

[4] Among New York City's various ethnic and racial groups, the degree of clustering differed greatly. The Irish Americans, except for a few areas (notably Hell's Kitchen on Manhattan's Mid-West Side), were dispersed (Rosenwaike 1972, 83).

surrounded by communities where other nationalities predominated. Although most of New York City's Little Italies are today largely devoid of Italian American residents, a vast material culture (churches, storefronts, generic buildings of all sorts) is often remarkably intact. While there was a remarkable degree of homogeneity in Little Italies everywhere in the United States, the histories of the Italian American communities were never identical.

When sorted out by Health Areas, the statistics on the distribution of ethnic groups collected by the 1930 Census show that most first- and second-generation Italian Americans congregated in the fifty-four, often contiguous, Health Areas where they comprised from 30 to 88 percent of the population. The density of the Italian American population varied: 5 Health Areas (four in Manhattan and one in the Bronx) more than 75 percent; 18 from 50 to 74.9 percent; 31 from 30 to 49.9 percent (Shedd 1934, 4). The straight lines and right angles of the Health Areas' boundaries were not coterminous with the "natural" boundaries of the city's Little Italies. The Little Italies overflowed the Health Areas' artificial boundaries. While the majority of the city's Italian American residents lived in Little Italies, most of the balance of the Italian American populace resided in ethnically mixed Health Areas adjacent to these solidly Italian American areas. The absence of large numbers of Italian Americans in the other Health Areas is the other side of the coin—during this period, there were many Health Areas where the Italian population dropped to 3 percent or even less. In Manhattan, these included Health Areas located on both the Upper East Side and the Upper West Side as well as heavily Jewish and Irish American Inwood at the northern tip of Manhattan. Brooklyn, the Bronx, and Queens also had many Health Areas with very few Italian Americans; eight of Staten Island's nine Health Areas had significant Italian American populations (Shedd 1934, 4, 9; Health Center 1944, 98, 192-294).

Throughout the United States, from about 1910 until 1950, Italians had the highest degree of residential self-segregation of any European-derived nationality (Yans-McLoughlin 1971, 116). The harsh economic realities of the Great Depression heightened the high levels of residential density found among Italian Americans. Although less documented than the other two clustering groups, Jews and African Americans, prejudice also played a very real, albeit immeasurable, role in limiting the dispersal, much less the assimilation, of Italian Americans. From 1930 to 1940, with the exception of some areas of original settlement, where demolition of aged residential buildings occurred, decreases in the "Italian" presence were rare. An especially large increase (from 38 to 50 percent) in the "Italian" population occurred in the Bushwick Health District Center 1944 (Health Center 1944, 140).

The densest concentration of Italian Americans in New York City was found in Manhattan's Mulberry Street Little Italy, the city's oldest Little Italy, where in 1930, 88.2 percent of its residents were first- and second-generation Italian American. Among the fourteen Health Areas in the Lower West Health Center District, Mulberry Street shared the distinction of having the lowest median monthly rent ($24) with an adjacent Health Area that included Chinatown and a mixed, predominantly Irish American tenement district in Hell's Kitchen on Manhattan's Mid-West Side. In the broadest sense, these low rents reflected meager family incomes. In 1930, 16.5 percent of this Little Italy's families had no adult wage earners working full time; this alarming figure rose by 1932 to an astounding 47.6 percent. Mulberry Street ceded first place in the category "number of persons per room" to the adjacent Health Area 68 encompassing the South Village, whose Italian American population reached 69 percent. The two Health Areas embracing Greenwich Village (68 and 64) had low monthly rents but only slightly higher-than-average rates of unemployment. These anomalous data speak to some special characteristics of this Little Italy, which unlike most other Little Italies has been well documented (Ware 1994; Tricarico 1984; Health Center 1944, 86-88).

The Great Depression reversed the Italian Americans' painfully slow economic progress. The economic catastrophe of the early 1930s had other, more complex, outcomes—it reinforced the Little Italies, which contained abundant supplies of cheap housing. Throughout the Depression, the increasing practice of households doubling up and the decreasing number of new-household formation dramatically depressed the rental market (Cohen 1993, 42). The predominance of evidence indicates the further consolidation of the cities' Little Italies; their borders expanded and their populations increased.

EMERGENCE OF A DISTINCTIVE CULTURE

The most salient feature of the New York City's Italian American settlement was its concentration in Little Italies; densely populated, low-rent, working class districts, where a distinctive, hybrid culture germinated. In addition to its powerful symbols and compelling practices, the culture was expressed linguistically. In 1934, *The Italians of New York* reported, "The constant intermingling of Italians from various provinces composed a new composite jargon . . . [that] infiltrated English words . . . to create a new Esperanto of Italian dialects" (Federal Writers' Project 1934, 22). Recently, Nancy Carnevale explained that the Napolitano dialect dominated this conglomerate of Italian dialects, which over time synthesized with elements of Standard Italian, Standard English and Italianized English (Carnevale 2011, 36). This hybrid language's development was interrupted by a series of events discussed later in this essay, so that it did not have the opportunity to produce significant literature.

Whatever the "outsiders" thought about Italian Americans and their communities, within their boundaries the residents themselves valued their distinct lifestyle with its attendant value system. The phenomenon of Italian Americans' residential concentration accompanied by a distinctive lifestyle was not peculiar to New York City. Everywhere Southern Italians settled in America they founded Little Italies.

These densely concentrated, multi-generational communities contained everything needed for their lives—Italian national churches,[5] specialty food stores (Cinotto 2002, 229-257), home-town clubs, social and athletic clubs—except enough jobs. However, almost always America's Little Italies arose in areas close to employment or to public transportation leading to places of employment. No less important, the Little Italies' population density allowed for the intense social experiences their members sought. Two scholars recently described the Little Italies as "archival spaces where *tutto parle*: the streets, the buildings, the market stands, the statues of saints, the signs in the shop windows, people's dress . . . [It is] a primal scene, a total social fact, where history and demography meet to fashion a cultural standpoint" (Boelhower and Rocco Pallone 1999, vii).[6] In the midst of the New York metropolis and in towns and cities across

---

[5] In the New York Metropolitan Area, from 1866 to 1961, the Catholic Church established seventy-four Italian "national" parishes, which created spaces inviting the use of the Italian language and the practice of typical aspects of Italian folk religious practices, most consequentially, the *feste* (Tomasi 1975, 99).

[6] Based on his research on Chicago's Little Italies, Vecoli underscored "the degree to which the *contadini* succeeded in reconstructing their native towns in the heart of industrial Chicago" (Vecoli 1964, 408). Less sanguinely, Silvio Tomasi viewed the Little Italies as, "tentative and temporary substitutes for the Old World community" (Tomasi, *Power and Piety*, 38).

the United States, Southern Italians' re-created their *paese*, which Rudolf Vecoli alternately called "rural cities" or "hill towns," their ancestral homes where they had lived and from which, on a daily basis, they traveled to their fields (Vecoli 2064, p 405-405).

Italian American families' housing choices were not entirely determined by their income levels; at least equally, they also spoke to their heartfelt need for participation in an adapted Southern Italian lifestyle. The Little Italies constituted an environment where Southern Italian immigrants were able to satisfy many of their cultural—even spiritual—needs. Similarly, the Italian immigrants' consumption patterns reflected the materialization of their primary value of strengthening family solidarity. How they made their money reflected their experiences in Southern Italy; how they spent their money re-enacted the mores of their land of origin. Italian Americans' social and economic profile presented impediments to their acculturation (Cinotto 2010, 11).

The family-based value system could only be maintained and transmitted to the succeeding generation through families. Endogamy became both a cause and a consequence of this culture. In 1927, 970 of every one thousand marriages of Italian American women were with an Italian American man. (The rate of in-marriage for Italian men, 828 per thousand, was lower because more men than woman emigrated from Italy to America, thereby creating a shortage of marriageable Italian women.) Covello suggests that in those instances when Italians intermarried the children were raised in Italian American communities, where "the impact of an Italian cultural pattern greatly off sets the infiltration of American norms" (Covello 1945, 33-35; Carpenter 1927, 234-245). One scholar of the Italian American experience observed that until the gigantic mobilization of military and civilians on behalf of the war effort began, "Italian Americana was vast and almost incomprehensible. [It was] insular and insulated" (Mormino 2007, 12, 13). Little Italies, however, were not counterfeit versions of Southern Italian *paese*. While they incorporated many features of the latter they were adaptive, hybrid phenomena, where a nascent Italian American culture evidenced its potential for mobilizing its residents for a politics that asserted their economic *and* social (including cultural) needs (Meyer 2011, 166-173; Cinotto 2002, 347).

POLITICS

A form of inarticulate solidarity defined the ethos of these inward-looking communities. When affirmed, this culture could support—even embrace—the wider solidarity of the New Deal and even further Left manifestations. Nowhere was that more evident than in New York City's largest Little Italy—Italian Harlem. Rudolph Vecoli averred that they created urban environments where at least "for a time . . . their [residents'] dual identities as proletarians and as Italians were congruent sources of solidarity" (Vecoli 2003, 51). In short, far from being obstacles to political mobilization, these closely-knit communities were sites for political action opposed to the possessive individualism incubated by American exceptionalism.[7]

While experiencing an extraordinary degree of distress, New York's Little Italies simultaneously served as sites of political and cultural assertion. The crisis resulted in a political mobilization of Italian Americans into the New Deal coalition. The Italian Americans had massive participation in New Deal work programs (most notably the Work Projects Administration [WPA]) and benefited from the full array of its other social and economic interventions, from minimum-wage regulation to the stipends the National Youth Act awarded to high-school students. The New Deal gave Italian Americans a substantial stake in political outcomes at every level of government. Italian Americans further bonded with Roosevelt when in his second inaugural address he focused on the plight of the one-third of the population that was ill-housed, ill-clad, and ill-nourished. New York's Italian Americans' political mobilization was most fully realized in Italian Harlem where the radical congressman Vito Marcantonio and the educational theorist and practitioner Leonard Covello synthesized a social-democratic politics and cultural-pluralist ethos that embodied an alternative paradigm of American democracy. Their vision fused individual legal/political rights guaranteed by the U.S. Constitution, along with economic and cultural rights.

Vito Marcantonio (and Fiorello La Guardia) enrolled in the American Labor Party (ALP) at its first registration in 1937. A higher percentage of

---

[7] This essay takes issue with the Lizabeth Cohen's thesis, as developed in *Making a New Deal*, that posits that progressive politics, which she terms "welfare capitalism," was made possible by the demise of "ethnic provincialism," brought about by the Great Depression's destruction of the ethnic infrastructure, and most especially the mutual-aid societies (Cohen 1990, 5, 13, 211, 253; Cinotto 2009, 283-285).

New York's Italian Americans voted for the ALP than any other European-derived group except for the Jews who provided its major base (Meyer 1997, 34-47; Bayor 1988, 41). Left-led unions provided political arenas which enabled many members of the city's Italian American communities to absorb and express Left politics. While the history of the "Italian" locals of the International Ladies Garment Workers' Union has been well documented, the relationship of New York City's overwhelmingly working-class Italian American community to the Communist-led unions has yet to find its scholars. *The Fur and Leather Worker*, the monthly publication of what was the most openly Communist union in the United States, documents an integral relationship between this union and its Italian American membership. The union's International-Secretary Pietro Lucchi and members of its Executive Board of this 110,000 member union were Italian Americans. Furthermore, the union newspaper promoted the candidacies of its Italian American members who ran on the ALP line. Most significantly, at least one page of *The Fur and Leather Worker* was printed in Italian. Needless to say, the publication regularly featured Marcantonio's activities as well as the painstaking efforts of the union to ensure his reelections.

The national profile of Italian Americans, to a heightened degree, matched those of the core components of the New Deal coalition: working class, first- and second-generation European-derived national groups, who along with the African Americans provided the mass base for the New Deal, outside the American South. The Republican Party's Catholic-baiting campaign against Alfred E. Smith in 1928 caused Italian Americans (as it did for all Catholic ethnic groups and the Jews) to flock to the Democratic Party. Among the European ethnic groups, Smith's Italian American vote (77 percent) was among the highest. In 1932, of all the ethnic and racial groups in urban areas, only Jews voted for Roosevelt in higher percentages (91 percent) than Italian Americans (88 percent). In tandem with Roosevelt's smaller pluralities from his unprecedented landslide in 1936, nationally the Italian American vote for Roosevelt in 1940 decreased to 75 percent, which was equal to the percentage of Roosevelt's Irish American vote, though far less than his 89 percent tally from the Jews. The Italian American vote was not solely an ethnic vote; in 1940, for example, 77 percent of poor Italian Americans, but only 61 percent of Italian Americans with average incomes, voted for Roosevelt. The movement of the Italians away from FDR in 1940 has been exaggerated and was mostly limited to NYC.

The Italian American vote for Roosevelt closely paralleled the Italian American vote nation wide. In 1932, the "Italian" vote for Roosevelt (80.5) was the highest of all ethnic groups. (Until the funding of the ALP many Jews continued to vote Socialist; hence, their lower 72.2 percent vote for Roosevelt.) In 1936 the "Italian" vote for Roosevelt fell very slightly to 78.7 percent (Bayor 1988, 147). The tremendous drop in the "Italian" vote for Roosevelt in 1940 (42.2 percent) had multiple causes and did not recover in 1944. These drastic decreases were not duplicated in Italian communities elsewhere. It was only after the war that the New York City "Italians" resumed voting for Democrats in numbers similar to other European-derived groups.

The political awakening of New York's Italian Americans was linked to the extraordinary victories of the first and second of Fiorello La Guardia's three election campaigns, the city's first Italian American mayor. The Italian vote was critical for La Guardia's success in all three races. La Guardia had uniquely successful administrations, which in January 1933 began the first of three four-year terms, a period roughly coterminous with Roosevelt's thirteen-year-long presidency (Bayor 1988, 130).

ITALIAN HARLEM

Italian Harlem was located east of Park Avenue in East Harlem, a 253-block area whose streets were organized in an unmodified grid pattern, bounded on the east by the East River, on the west by Fifth Avenue, on the south by East 96th Street, and the north by East 125th Street. The core of Italian Harlem consisted of three contiguous Health Areas (26, 21, and 22) with Italian American populations ranging from 78.6 to 84.3 percent. The so-called "natural area" of Italian Harlem spilled over the boundaries of the three core Health Areas into the six neighboring Health Areas, whose Italian American population ranged from 10.6 to 47 percent (Shedd 1934, 3, 9). Including third-generation Italian Americans, the "Italian" population of Italian Harlem was approximately 150,000 (Federal Writers' Project 1938, 21). Italian Harlem was also the most "Italian" of the city's Little Italies; it was a community where Southern Italian folkways and mores persisted in some very conspicuous ways. During the 1930's, the *feste* dedicated to Our Lady of Mount Carmel, by far the largest such celebration in the United States, served as a magnet for throngs, from near and wide, who sought miraculous cures from the *Madonna* and the opportunity to assert their *italianità* (Orsi 1985, 85). In "Contadini in Chicago," Vecoli noted, "The persistence of Old World customs among the south Italians was perhaps best exemplified by the *feste...*" (Vecoli 1964, 416).

Italian Harlem's residents were unusually poor—even when compared with other Italian American communities. In 1940, in New York City when the median monthly rent was $38, the median monthly rents in Italian Harlem's three core Health Areas ranged from a low of $21 to a high of $24. The rate of Italian Harlem's adults who were unemployed or working for WPA ranged from 37 to nearly 42 percent (Health Center 1944, 74).

Donna Gabbacia has described the culture of the Little Italies as "defensive" (Gabaccia 2000, 191). In contrast with this generality, Italian Harlem provided a potential base for an assertive politics. From 1922, when Fiorello La Guardia began the first of his five congressional terms, to the defeat of seven-term Congressman Vito Marcantonio in 1950 by James Donovan (coalition candidate of the Democratic, Republican, and Liberal parties), Italian Harlem's electorate embraced a social democratic politics largely unfamiliar in the American political arena. As national spokespersons, La Guardia and his protégé Marcantonio advocated remarkably leftist agendas. They blended a general progressive program with unequaled eloquence for the specific interests of their Italian American, Puerto Rican, and African American constituents and immigrants and workers in general (Zinn 1958; Meyer 1989, 112-143; Rubinstein 2002). More than any other New York City Little Italy, Italian Harlem adopted political and organizational forms which effectively mobilized its members to address community needs.

Italian Harlem was also the home base and the social laboratory for Leonard Covello, arguably the single most important figure of the Italian American experience in the interwar years. The culmination of the extraordinarily fruitful career of Leonard Covello was his development of community-centered education, a strategy intended to meet the academic needs of Italian and other cultural-minority students and a bridge between the school and the community. As founding principal from 1934 until his retirement in 1956, he implemented a cultural-pluralist, social-activist curriculum for Benjamin Franklin High School (Covello 1958; Johanek and Puckett 2008). The ethos of Benjamin Franklin led the coauthors of a recently published book about this school to choose the subtitle: *Education as if Democracy Really Matters* (Johanek and Puckett 2007). Benjamin Franklin was dedicated to developing, "an informed, active citizenry equipped with knowledge, skills, and disposition to participate in cooperative activity that would incorporate the contributions of diverse cultural groups, even groups in conflict, to solve trenchant community problems" (Venturini, 2002, 73).[8]

Marcantonio and Covello's influence was solidified through their leadership in mobilizing the community to resolve the community's problems (Meyer 1985; Meyer 2008; Meyer 2003). Marcantonio and Covello's rootedness in Italian Harlem—they lived in adjacent row houses on East 116th Street (the community's *passeggiata*)—and vast service to the community kept at bay the pro-Fascist and clericalist forces, which in the 1930s gained power in many other Italian American communities. The awakening of Italian Harlem's latent political potential depended on two major factors: Italian Harlem's large population allowed for a complete community to develop, and its distinctly middle-class area (along East 116th Street and Pleasant Avenue) that comfortably housed a significant stratum of professionals and businessmen. In short, Italian Harlem was both large enough to constitute districts (congressional, state senatorial and assembly), and afforded an environment for individuals to reside who were capable of transforming the resentments and the dormant humanism of the community into a progressive outlook (Meyer 2008; Meyer 1999).

Two interrelated successful campaigns, which responded to the community's needs and embodied ideological assumptions of the New Deal, amplified the effects of these political activities. Through the efforts of Marcantonio, LaGuardia, and Covello, Benjamin Franklin, the first high school in East Harlem, then home to 209,000 residents, was constructed in 1934 in the heart of Italian Harlem. They also collaborated on a community-wide campaign to address Italian Harlem's woefully substandard housing. Completed in 1941, East River Houses, the United States' first high-rise public housing project, established an ethnically integrated community of 1,170 households that combined six city blocks into one

---

[8] The Office of War Information produced *A Better Tomorrow*, a film depicting the school as an exemplar of "democracy in action," which was screened to audiences of United States servicemen and civilians throughout Europe. "Community Mass Meeting," program of Oct. 8, 1945 assembly at Benjamin Franklin High School, Pennsylvania Historical Society, Covello Collection: Box 54, Folder 13 [CC, B, F]; Johanek and Puckett 2009).

super-block that allowed for a park-like setting facing the East River (Plunz 1990, 243-245; Cinotto 2009). These political campaigns tapped into the community spirit of an ethnic group that had been regularly described as "amoral familists" incapable of participating in collective activities for the commonweal. These developments tremendously enhanced the community's self-confidence and self-consciousness.

Italian Harlem's political life was energized by Marcantonio's spectacular political campaigns, which entailed frequent street-corner rallies that entailed a type of political theater, and massive election-eve assemblies at his so-called "Lucky Corner" (the northeast corner of East 116th Street and Lexington Avenue), whose inclusion of music and decorative lighting caused these political manifestations to resemble *feste*. The large-scale delivery of services to constituents by the Vito Marcantonio Political Association gave Italian Harlem's residents further evidence of the efficaciousness of political engagement (Meyer 1989, 15, 39, 101-106).[9]

The ideological assumptions of the Left New Deal combined with effective leadership and organization presented Italian Harlem's denizens an attractive alternative to the influence of the reigning troika of *prominenti*, Roman Catholic clergy, and philo-Fascists. The latter forces who, despite significant opposition, had gained hegemony over most Italian American communities, met their match in Italian Harlem (Pernicone, 2005, 124-208; Meyer 2007).

CONCLUSION

On the face of it, the shift of large sectors of New York City's Italian American community to the Left should not be surprising. The city's Italian American unemployed disproportionately benefited from New Deal programs, as did its 400,000 Italian American wage earners from its subsequent implementation of wage-and-hours regulations, such as the inauguration of a minimum wage, the eight-hour day, and overtime pay. The profile of New York's Italian Americans, to a heightened degree, matched that of the core components of the New Deal coalition: largely urban, working-class, first- and second-generation European-derived national groups, who, along with African Americans, provided the mass base for the New Deal, outside the American South. The political-cultural

---

[9] Marcantonio's delivery of services to constituents was legendary: from 1946 to 1948, his Congressional District's staff recorded 35,000 personal requests that had been attended to. (Meyer 1989, 88).

agenda that developed in Italian Harlem was congruent with its socio-economic reality (Meyer 1997; Meyer 2003).

The nationalist upsurge in New York City's Italian American communities engendered by Italy's invasion of Ethiopia in October 1935 loosened their embrace of the New Deal. Italy's declaration of war against the United States on December 11, 1941 had an even greater deleterious effect. In 1940 the Smith Act had branded 600,000 unnaturalized Italians as "aliens of enemy nationality." In the House of Representatives, Vito Marcantonio was one of only four Congressmen to vote against the bill and the only one to speak against its passage (Rubinstein 2002, 129-139). Although ultimately the Federal government interned only 250 Italian Americans, government policy stigmatized the entire community. It cast over Italian American families a pall of obloquy and insecurity. In addition to registering as resident aliens (as required by the Smith Act), unnaturalized Italian Americans could no longer own shortwave radios, cameras, or firearms; in addition they had to report to their local police any travel beyond their hometown, and at all times they were required to carry on their person an "enemy-alien registration card."[10] While on Columbus Day 1942 Roosevelt's shrewdly timed Presidential decree lifted these odious impositions, this trauma caused the Italian American community to embrace ever more rapidly what Covello termed the "coercive acculturation of Americanization," something they had hitherto stubbornly resisted.

In part as an assertion of their loyalty to the country of their birth, Italian American youth flooded armed forces recruitment centers. The war precipitated massive mobilizations for staffing the armed forces and war-materials production, which led to widespread social dislocations. Gary Mormino reminds his readers that one of five Italian Americans participated in these vast wartime movements. During the war, Italian Americans boys had often said farewell to their families in Italian; on their return, they most often left behind the language. The GI Bill-generated postwar opportunities (tuition grants and highly subsidized home mortgages) also encouraged the adoption of middle-class lifestyles by the hitherto proletarianized Italian Americans. The massive postwar flight to the suburbs fatally undermined the Little Italies everywhere in America.

---

[10] The largest number of Italian Americans affected by these restrictions lived in California; in San Francisco, the Federal government seized the fishing boat of Joe Di Maggio's father, Giuseppe (Cannistraro and Meyer 2003, 23-24).

The hollowing out of the Little Italies disrupted the distinctive family- and community-oriented Italian American lifestyle. The study and use of the Italian language fell precipitously.

The post-war political repression, whose most immediate effects were the obliteration of the American Left, including its relatively weak Italian American branch, struck the final blow (Meyer 2003, 205-227). Triumphant reaction and Cold War liberalism entailed Nativist cultural premises antithetical to the distinctive culture of the Little Italies. The humanistic (even materialistic) anthems such as *The House I Live In* and *America the Beautiful* lost out to the religiously strident *God Bless America* and an unsingable national anthem. The prevalent jingoistic Americanism obliterated the environment requisite for cultural pluralism. (Meyer 2008, 43-49). The loss of this alternative model of Italian Americana constituted losses for Italian Americans as well as for members of other minority cultures; these losses also coarsened the dominant culture which was no longer enriched and challenged by a more familial, communal ethos germinating in this vast archipelago of alternate communities. The hegemonic version of Italian American experience that exalted the ever-accelerating onward- and-upward entry of Italian Americans into the American mainstream fails to take into account its underside: which, for lack of a better term, is rank Americanization.

Paradoxically, for the Italian American community, the long decade of the 1930s (October 29, 1929 to December 7, 1941) was simultaneously a period of great privation and the moment of its greatest possibilities. During the Great Depression, a highly concentrated Italian American population had developed a cohesive culture to the point where simultaneously it could effectively function within the wider society, while maintaining an extraordinary degree of familial and communal solidarity. Thus, the Italian American community of this period offered an alternative to the ethos of possessive individualism, relentlessly marketed as "liberty." From this perspective, the 1930s represented the moment for New York City's Italian American community when it had the best chance to develop into an exemplary component of a pluralistic, democratic society, the promise of which, when not entirely forgotten, is often besmirched.

REFERENCES

Alba, Richard. *Italian Americans: The Twilight of Ethnicity.* New York: Prentice Hall, 1985.

Bayor, Ronald. *Neighbors in Conflict: The Irish, Germans, Jews and Italians of New York City, 1929-1941.* Second edition. Chicago: University of Illinois Press, 1988.

Berkowitz, Michael. "Americanization and Ethnicity in an Italian Community: Immigrants, Education, and Politics in East Harlem, 1920-1941." Senior Thesis, Princeton University, 1987.

Boelhower, William and Rocco Pallone, eds. "Introduction." In *Adjusting Sites: New Essays in Italian American Studies.* Stony Brook, NY: Filibrary, 1999.

Bureau of the Census, Fifteenth Census of the United States, 1930: Special Report on Foreign-Born White Families.

Cannistraro, Philip. "Understanding America." In *Italian Socialism: Between Politics and History*, edited by Spencer Di Scala. Amherst, MA: University of Massachusetts Press, 1996. 177-182.

_____. "The Italians of New York: An Historical Overview." In *The Italians of New York: Five Centuries of Struggle and Achievement*, edited by Philip Cannistraro. New York: New York Historical Society, 1999. 1-20.

Cannistraro, Philip and Gerald Meyer. "Italian American Radicalism: An Interpretive Essay." In *The Lost World of Italian American Radicalism.* Edited by Cannistraro and Meyer. Westport, CT: Praeger, 2002. 1-50.

Carnevale, Nancy. *A New Language, A New World: Italian Immigrants in the United States, 1890-1945.* Chicago: University of Illinois Press, 2009.

Carpenter, Niles. *Immigrants and Their Children.* Washington DC, 1927.

Caviaoli, Frank. "Patterns of Italian Immigration to America." In *Italian Americans in the Third Millennium: Social Histories and Cultural Representations*, edited by Paolo Giordano and Anthony Tamburri. New York: American Italian Historical Association, 2009. 1-18.

Cinotto, Simone. *Una famiglia che mangia insieme: cibe ed ethicità nella comunità italoamericana di New York, 1920-1940.* Torino, Italy: Otto editore, 2002.

_____. "Italian Americans and Public Housing in New York, 1937-1941: Cultural Pluralism, Ethnic Materialism, and the Welfare State." In *Democracy and Social Rights in the"Two Wests,"* edited by Alice Kessler-Harris and Maurizio Vaudagna. Torino, Italy: Collana Novo Americana, 2009. 279-306.

_____. "All Things Italian: Italian American Consumers and the Commodification of Difference." *VIA (Voices in Italian Americana)* 21.1 (2010).

Cohen, Lizabeth. *Making a New Deal: Industrial Workers in Chicago, 1919-1939.* New York: Cambridge University Press, 1990.

Cohen, Miriam. *Two Generations of Italian Women in New York City, 1900-1950.* Ithaca, NY: Cornell University Press, 1993.

Cordasco, Frederico. "Introduction." In Covello, Leonard. *The Social Background of the Italo-American School Child: A Study of the Southern Italian Family Mores and Their Effect on the School Situation in Italy and America.* Leiden, Netherlands: E. J. Brill, 1967. Xii-xxiv.

Covello, Leonard. *The Italians in America: A Brief Survey of a Sociological Research Program of Italo-American Communities, Bulletin Number 6.* New York: Casa Italiana Educational Bureau, Columbia University, 1934.

_____. "The Italians of New York." 1945. Unpublished manuscript in possession of Gerald Meyer.

_____. *The Heart Is the Teacher.* New York: McGraw Hill, 1958.

_____. *The Social Background of the Italo-American School Child: A Study of the Southern Italian Family Mores and Their Effect on the School Situation in Italy and America.* Leiden, Netherlands: E. J. Brill, 1967.

D'Alesandre, John. *Occupational Trends of Italians in New York City, Bulletin Number 8.* New York: Casa Italiana Educational Bureau, Columbia University, 1935.

Denning, Michael. *The Cultural Front: The Laboring of American Culture in the Twentieth Century.* New York: Verso, 1997.

Dittman, Michael. "The Federal Writers' Project and the Creation of Hegemony." *49th Parallel: An Interdisciplinary Journal of North American Studies* (Spring 1999): np.

Federal Writers' Project. *The Italians of New York: A Survey.* New York: Random House, 1938.

Gabaccia, Donna. *From Sicily to Elizabeth Street: Housing and Social Change among Italian Immigrants, 1880-1930.* Albany, NY: SUNY Press, 1984.

_____. *Migrants and Militants: Rural Sicilians Become American Workers.* New Brunswick, NJ: Rutgers University Press, 1988.

_____. *Italy's Many Diasporas.* Seattle, WA: University of Washington State Press, 2000.

Greenberg, Cheryl Lynn. *"Or Does It Explode?": Black Harlem in the Great Depression.* New York: Oxford University Press, 1991.

Guglielmo, Jennifer. *Living the Revolution: Italian Women's Resistance and Radicalism in New York City, 1880-1945.* Chapel Hill, NC: University of North Carolina Press, 2010.

New York City Department of Health and Neighborhood Development. *Health Center Districts, New York Handbook of Statistical Reference Data: Ten-Year Period, 1931-1940.* New York, 1944.

Johanek, Michael and John Puckett. *Leonard Covello and the Making of Benjamin Franklin High School: Education as if Citizenship Mattered.* Philadelphia: Temple University Press, 2007.

Lapomarda, Vincent. "Press: Italian American." In *The Italian American Experience: An Encyclopedia,* edited by Salvatore LaGumina, et al. New York: Garland Publishers, 2000. 509-518.

Luconi, Stefano. "The Italian Americans and the New Deal Coalition." In WWW.Transatlantica.org/document212html. 2006.

Mangione, Jerre. *The Dream and the New Deal: The Federal Writers' Project, 1935-1943.* New York: Avon Books, 1972.

Meyer, Gerald. "Leonard Covello and Vito Marcantonio: A Lifetime of Collaboration for Progress." *Italica* 62.1 (1985): 54-66.

_____. *Vito Marcantonio: Radical Politician, 1902-1954.* Albany, NY: SUNY Press, 1989.

_____. "The American Labor Party and New York City's Italian American Communities." In *Industry, Technology, Labor and the Italian American Communities,* edited by Mario Aste, et al. Staten Island, NY: American Italian Historical Association, 1997. 33-49.

_____. "Italian Americans and the American Communist Party." In *The Lost World of Italian American Radicalism,* edited by Philip Cannistraro and Gerald Meyer. Westport, CT: Praeger Publishers, 2002. 205-227.

_____. "When Sinatra Came to Italian Harlem: The 1945 'Race Riot' at Benjamin Franklin High School." In *Are Italians White? How Race Is Made in America,* edited by Jennifer Guglielmo and Salvatore Salerno. New York: Routledge, 2003. 161-176.

_____. "Cultural Pluralist Response to Americanization: Horace Kallen, Randolph Bourne, Louis Adamic, and Leonard Covello." *Socialism and Democracy* 22.3 (2008): 19-51.

_____. "Carlo Tresca: The Dilemma of an Anti-Communist Radical." *Altreitalie* 34 (2007): 94-111.

_____. "Theorizing Italian American History: The Search for an Historiographical Paradigm." In *The Status of Interpretation in Italian American Studies,* edited by Jerome Krase. Stony Brook, NY: Forum Italicum Publishing, 2011. 166-173.

Milione, Vincenzo and Christine Gambino. *Sí, Parliamo Italiano! Globalization of the Italian Culture in the United States.* New York: John D. Calandra Italian American Institute, 2009.

Mormino, Gary. " 'It's Not Personal, It's Professional': Italian Americans and World War II." In *The Impact of World War II on Italian Americans: 1935-Present*. New York: American Italian Historical Association, 2007. 7-10.

Orsi, Robert. *The Madonna of 115th Street: Faith and Community in Italian Harlem, 1889-1950*. New Haven, CT: Yale University Press, 1985.

Perlmann, Joel. *Ethnic Differences: Schooling and Social Structure among the Irish, Italians, Jews, and Blacks in an American City, 1880-1935*. New York: Cambridge University Press, 1995.

Pernicone, Nunzio. *Carlo Tresca: Portrait of a Rebel*. New York: Palgrave, 2005.

Plunz, Richard. *A History of Housing in New York*. New York: Columbia University Press, 1990.

Rosenwaike, Ira. *Population History of New York City*. Syracuse, NY: Syracuse University Press, 1972.

Rubinstein, Annette T. ed. *I Vote My Conscience: Debates, Speeches, and Writings of Vito Marcantonio, 1935-1950*. Second edition. New York: John D. Calandra Italian American Institute, 2002.

Shedd, William. *Italian Population in New York: Bulletin Number 4*. New York: Casa Italiana Educational Bureau, Columbia University, 1934.

Starr, Dennis. "Population." In *The Italian American Experience: An Encyclopedia*, edited by Salvatore LaGumina, et al. New York: Garland Publishing, 2000. 496-509.

Taylor, Nick. *American-Made: The Enduring Legacy of the WPA: When FDR Put the Nation to Work*. New York: Bantam Books, 2008.

Tomasi, Silvio. *Piety and Power: The Role of Italian Parishes in the New York Metropolitan Area*. Staten Island, NY: Center of Migration Study, 1975.

Tricarico, Donald. *The Italians of Greenwich Village: The Social Structure and Transformation of an Ethnic Community*. Staten Island, NY: Center of Migration Studies, 1984.

Vecoli, Rudolph. "*Contadini* in Chicago: A Critique of the Uprooted." *Journal of American History* 51 (December 1964): 404-417.

_____. "The Making and Un-making of the Italian American Working Class." In *The Lost World of Italian American Radicalism: Politics, Labor, Culture*, edited by Philip Cannistraro and Gerald Meyer. Westport, CT: Praeger, 2003. 51-75.

Venturini, Nadia. "Leonard Covello and Intercultural Education at Benjamin Franklin High School in the 1930s," *Italian American Review* 9.1 (2002): 73-110.

Wallace, James. "Patterns of Italian Immigration to America." In *Italian Americans in the Third Millennium: Social Histories and Cultural Representations*, edited by Paolo Giordano and Anthony Tamburri. New York: Bordighera, 2009. 29-54.

Ware, Caroline. *Greenwich Village, 1920-1930: A Comment on American Civilization in the Post-War Years.* Berkeley: University of California Press, 1994.

Wenger, Beth. *New York Jews and the Great Depression.* New Haven, CT: Yale University Press, 1996.

Yans-McLaughlin, Elizabeth. *Family and Community: Italian Immigrants in Buffalo, 1880-1930.* Ithaca, NY: Cornell University Press, 1971.

Zinn, Howard. *La Guardia in Congress.* New York: W. W. Norton, 1958.

The Lost—and Found—World of Italian American Radicalism

Marcella Bencivenni

In 1976 Paul Cowan, a *Village Voice* journalist researching the historic 1912 Lawrence Strike, came across the dramatic story of Cammella Teoli, an Italian girl who in 1911 had been scalped by a machine at the American Woolen Company mill where she worked. Like many children of impoverished Italian immigrants, Cammella began working when she was only thirteen after a labor recruiter persuaded her struggling father to forge her birth certificate so as to evade child-labor laws. It took her seven months of hospital care to recover from her accident. Upon her dismissal from the hospital, she joined the Lawrence strikers, and, when socialist Margaret Sanger arranged for her and other workers to appear before a congressional hearing on working conditions at the textile mills, her moving testimony prompted a federal investigation of American factories.[1]

Cammella's chilling story made front-page news and overnight she became a *cause célèbre*.[2] Yet to Cowan's astonishment, her own children knew nothing of their mother's heroic working-class past: they had heard neither of her accident (despite an odd bald spot on her scalp), nor of her sensational testimony in Washington, D.C.; they had no idea that she had been politically active at a very young age, much less that she had directly contributed to labor reforms.

Teoli's story is by now well known. Ever since Cowan published it, scholars have used her act of personal repression as a powerful example of submerged labor history and erasure from historical consciousness and

---

[1] Paul Cowan, "Introduction" to *Lawrence 1912: The Bread and Roses Strike* by William Cahn (New York: Pilgrim Press, 1982) and "A Town's Amnesia," *New York Times*, March 30, 1980, E21. Cammella's story is also recounted in Philip V. Cannistraro and Gerald Meyer, "Italian American Radicalism: An Interpretative History," in Cannistraro and Meyer, eds., *The Lost World of Italian American Radicalism: Politics, Labor and Culture* (Westport, CT: Praeger, 2003), 1-2.

[2] Her testimony has been reprinted in Joyce L. Kornbluh, *Rebel Voices: An IWW Anthology* (Chicago: Charles H. Kerr, 1998), 181-184.

memory.[3] Her narrative, wrote David Cohen in 1994, carried within it a number of issues and tensions that would define the work of historians over several years: the complexity of forgetting, the power in the locations and meaning of silences, the forces and patterns of suppression, the catharsis of commemoration, and, in essence, the production of history itself.[4]

This sense of a lost radical history has been a particularly important theme of Italian American studies, and, interestingly enough, it continues to define the field. Indeed, more than thirty years later, Teoli's story remains emblematic of a vanished radical past—what Philip Cannistraro aptly called "the lost world of Italian American radicalism" on the occasion of a groundbreaking conference he organized in New York City in 1997.

For years the radical chapter of Italian American history had been blatantly ignored. General surveys of the Italian American experience excluded any discussion of extremely popular radical leaders such as Carlo Tresca, Arturo Giovannitti, or Vito Marcantonio, and rarely spoke of the contributions of Italian workers to the American labor struggle of the early twentieth century.[5] Italian immigrants were typically portrayed as a homogenous mass of conservative, apathetic and apolitical people concerned only in the preservation of *la via vecchia* (the old way). This characterization derived in large part from the increasing identification, and self-identification, of Italian Americans with reactionary and conservative

---

[3] Most notably, Herbert Gutman, *Power and Culture: Essays on American Working Class* (New York: The New Press, 1992), 396.

[4] David William Cohen, *The Combing of History* (Chicago: University of Chicago Press, 1994), 4.

[5] The best example of this omission is Richard Gambino, *Blood of My Blood: The Dilemma of Italian Americans* (New York: Guernica, 1996; first edition 1974). See also: Erik Amfitheatrof, *The Children of Columbus* (Boston: Little Brown, 1973); Alexander DeConde, *Half Bitter, Half Sweet* (New York: Charles Scribner's Sons, 1971); Luciano Iorizzo and Salvatore Mondello, *The Italian Americans* (New York: Twayne Publishers, 1971), Humbert Nelli, *From Immigrant to Ethnic: The Italian Americans* (Boston: G.K. Hall, 1983); Andrew Rolle, *The American Italians: Their History and Culture* (Belmont, Ca.: Wodsworth, Pub. Co., 1972); and Allan Schoener, *The Italian Americans* (New York: MacMillan, 1987). None of them explores the subject of Italian American radicalism. Only Jerre Mangione and Ben Morreale's *La Storia: Five Centuries of the Italian American Experience* (New York: Harper, 1993) includes to some extent information of radicalism. For an alternative approach that incorporates radicalism see Irving Howe on the Jewish immigrant experience: *World of Our Fathers* (New York: Schocken Books, 1989; first edition 1976).

politics. But it also reflected the tenacious influence of Edward Banfied's theory of "amoral familism," advanced in late 1950s, according to which southern Italians were indifferent to anything and anyone outside their immediate family.[6]

The conference that Cannistraro organized in 1997 powerfully challenged these views. More than sixty scholars from across disciplines (including this author) showed that, contrary to popular perceptions, "leading figures and segments of the Italian American community—at times larger and more influential than at others—have been radical."[7] Sixteen of those papers were consequently published in 2003 in what would become Cannistraro's last book. Entitled, like the conference, *The Lost World of Italian American Radicalism: Politics Labor and Culture* and co-edited with Gerald Meyer, it offered a sweeping history of the Italian American radical experience from the late nineteenth century through the present. In addition to a fifty-page introduction by Cannistraro and Meyer which brilliantly synopsized the history of the movement, the book included new critical studies on women's political activism, contemporary Italian American radical literature, and the involvement of Italian Americans in the civil rights and student movements of the 1960s.

Although Cannistraro never conducted original research on Italian American radicalism, he long recognized the need to correct the omission of radicalism from the Italian American picture and rescue, in the words of his mentor, A. William Salomone, "those complicated and little worlds of Italian American radicalism" from historical oblivion. "What is at stake," he wrote with Meyer, "is both historical accuracy and Italian American self-perception."[8]

His first book on Italian American history, *The Italians of New York: Five Centuries of Struggle and Achievement,* was an anthology based on an exhibition by the same title he helped curate at the New-York Historical Society in 1999. Unlike other general histories of Italian Americans which completely ignored radicalism, *The Italians of New York* featured the radical experience prominently among its essays. Two out of the twelve articles included in the volume were specifically devoted to radicalism: Nunzio Pernicone's overview of political activism in New York City and Jennifer Guglielmo's analysis of Italian women's feminism and unionism.

---

[6] *The Moral Basis of a Backward Society* (New York: The Free Press, 1958).
[7] Cannistraro and Meyer, "Italian American Radicalism: An Interpretative History," 3.
[8] Ibid., 2, 3.

Fred Gardaphè's discussion of the Italian immigrant literary legacy also incorporated radical writers like Pietro di Donato, Carl Marzani, and Mario Fratti.[9]

Today, many other publications attest to the growing interest in the lost world of Italian American radicalism. Starting with the pioneering research of the late Rudolph Vecoli, Nunzio Pernicone, and Donna Gabaccia, scholars of Italian American history have forcefully challenged the early renditions of the Italian immigrant experience. A powerful counter-tale has gradually emerged showing that Italian Americans possess a vibrant, if "lost," radical past.

Recent contributions include two comparative volumes on the Italian radical diaspora, *Italian Workers of the World* (2001) edited by Donna Gabaccia and Fraser Ottanelli and *Women, Gender and Transnational Lives* (2003) edited by Donna Gabaccia and Franca Iacovetta; Michael Topp's *Those Without a Country* (2002), which studied the political culture of the Italian Socialist Federation; Nunzio Pernicone's sweeping biography of Carlo Tresca (2005); Jennifer Guglielmo's *Living the Revolution* (2010) which offered groundbreaking research on Italian women's political activism in New York; and my own book, *Italian Immigrant Radical Culture* (2011), based on my doctoral dissertation, which Cannistraro supervised and helped to conceive.

Thanks to this rich literature, we now know that, far from passive or apathetic, Italian immigrants formed anarchist, socialist, communist, and feminist groups wherever they settled; they created alternative newspapers; they founded their own separate unions; and they participated in the major industrial strikes of the early twentieth century, providing both leadership and mass militancy. We also now understand that despite Mussolini's strong popularity in the United States, not all Italian Americans succumbed to fascist rhetoric; in fact, Italian American resistance to Mussolini long predated the formation of the American Popular Front and was central in mobilizing opposition to fascism. We are also beginning to see, thanks above all to the work of Donna Gabaccia, Jennifer Guglielmo, and Waldron Merithew, that Italian immigrant women constituted a significant minority of the labor and radical movement, making important contributions as community organizers, strikers, and fundrais-

---

[9] Nunzio Pernicone, "Italian Immigrant Radicalism in New York," 77-92; Jennifer Guglielmo, Italian American Women's Activism in New York," 103-114; Fred Gardaphè, "Italian/American Writers of New York," 93-102.

ers, and also developing their own forms of female activism, which often operated in opposition to and outside of men's political world.[10]

Collectively the historiography points to the enormous richness and sectarianism of Italian American radicalism. But the emphasis on, and preoccupation with, the exceptional elements of each one of the leftist groups (anarchists, socialists, syndicalists, communists) have obscured their common culture and roots, resulting in a fragmented narrative of the radical experience.

There is no doubt that the *sovversivi*, as Italian radicals of all political persuasions were collectively called, diverged over issues of doctrine, the state, the role of unions, and their relationship regarding the American and the Italian Left. Despite frequent calls to unity, there also existed bitter rivalries among leaders and political groups that prevented even informal political accord. Yet, for all their differences, Italian radicals shared a distinctive worldview, a sensibility based on communal native traditions, ethical values, and political dreams. This common vision, as I suggest in my book, was an integral aspect of the movement. Not only did it provide the main source of inspiration, it also encapsulated a particular way of life and worldview.

Socialism, anarchism, syndicalism, and communism were more than political doctrines; they were part of a larger *Weltanschauung* or vision — what Italian radicals called "the beautiful ideal," the revolutionary dream of working class emancipation and social justice. Surfacing repeatedly in the *sovversivi*'s speeches and writings, this common ideal reflected an important ethical dimension of the movement which, I believe, has been overlooked by the factionalism that split it. It was a vision deeply rooted in a humanistic conception of life and a disarming idealism and messianic faith in a "beautiful tomorrow" when love, peace and social justice would reign for every woman and man on earth.[11]

To disseminate their message, the *sovversivi* created a multitude of subsidiary institutions and sponsored a wide range of cultural and recreational activities that shaped the movement's political culture and at the

---

[10] See for example Donna Gabaccia and Franca Iacovetta, eds., *Women, Gender and Transnational Lives: Italian Workers of the World* (Toronto: University of Toronto Press, 2002); and Jennifer Guglielmo, *Living the Revolution. Italian Women's Resistance and Radicalism in New York City, 1880-1945* (Chapel Hill: The University of North Carolina Press, 2010).

[11] Cf. Marcella Bencivenni, *Italian Immigrant Radical Culture: The Idealism of the Sovversivi in the United States, 1890-1940* (New York: New York University Press, 2011), 44.

same time enriched the social life of the immigrant community. They formed evening and Sunday schools that drew on the Italian socialist experience of *Università Popolari* (people's universities). They created countless educational circles and self-organized radical bookstores, *librerie rosse*, that made hundreds of books and pamphlets (both nonfiction and fiction) available to workers. They had their own orchestras, choruses, and dramatic societies that sponsored weekly performances in local bars, circles, or hired halls. They arranged special dances, concerts, picnics, and annual festivals such as the *festa della frutta*, a peasant custom held each autumn to celebrate the fall harvest. In place of traditional national and religious holidays, they established their own revolutionary celebrations, such as May Day, the international workers' day, and March 18, the anniversary of the Paris Commune. They sponsored conferences and lectures; published hundreds of newspapers; and produced dozens of pamphlets, poems, social dramas, drawings, and cartoons.[12]

Complementing the existing scholarship, my research brings attention to this rich oppositional culture and the way cultural traditions, institutions, literature and art fused with, and sustained, political work. In particular, I tried to salvage the literary dimension of the movement, a dimension that despite its richness has not been adequately studied.

Take, for example, radical poetry. Its prominence in the culture of Italian immigrant radicals is evident by the pages of their newspapers which are filled with verses and songs often embellished with drawings and occasionally published on the first page or in small pamphlets similar to the "little red song books" popularized by the Industrial Workers of the World. Some poems by famous Italian social poets, like Pietro Gori's "Primo Maggio" or Mario Rapisardi's "Canto del Mietatore," were published so often that they could be considered official anthems of the *sovversivi*'s culture.

The high number of Italian American radical poets is also suggestive of the importance of poetry in the world of the *sovversivi*. In the course of my research, I have identified at least 14 poets who regularly composed verses for radical newspapers between 1900 and 1930, but many others, I am sure, await discovery.[13] A number of them, like Arturo Giovannitti,

---

[12] Ibid., 2-3.

[13] Arturo Giovannitti is the most famous example, but other poets include: Francesco Greco, Pietro Greco, Efrem Bartoletti, Francesco Pitea, Alessandro Sisca better known with his pen name of Riccardo Cordiferro, Bellalma Forzato Spezia, Virgilia D'Andrea, Antonino

Efrem Bartoletti, Virgilia D'Andrea and Francesco Greco, published several volumes of poetry and earned a considerable reputation among the Italian immigrant workers in the United States as bards of the poor and oppressed. Yet, aside from Giovannitti, the *sovversivi*'s poetry has been completely, consciously or unconsciously, ignored—buried in the pages of equally forgotten radical newspapers.

While overlooked today, these verses fired the hopes and dreams of thousands of demoralized Italian immigrant workers. They not only gave eloquent voice to the working-class struggle of the early twentieth century but they also best captured the idealism and passion that moved the *sovversivi*: their commitment to the revolution, their hatred of privilege and abuse, and above all their profound devotion to the ideal of human redemption—"the stubborn dream of peace and love," in the words of the anarchist poetess Virgilia D'Andrea.

The theatre was another fascinating aspect of the lost world of Italian American radicalism. *Filodrammatiche rosse*, Italian dramatic societies affiliated with radical groups, were formed in the United States as early as 1895 and continued to operate until World War II, putting on hundreds of plays, ranging from European and Italian classics to original productions written by Italian American radicals.[14] The radical stage occupied a very special and important place in the Italian immigrant communities, entertaining the workers and helping to promote radicalism. Indeed, next to the press, it was the most important vehicle of propaganda and education, as well as the primary source of income for radical papers and other political activities.[15]

Filodrammatiche rosse did not differ much from other theatres. Their major role was to entertain Italian American workers, providing a space where they could satisfy their social needs and escape the hardship of

---

Crivello, Nino Caradonna, Vittorio Vidali, Simpicio Righi, Giuseppe Zappulla, and Onorio Ruotolo.

[14] Among the favorite Italian authors were Paolo Giacometti, Giovanni Verga, Felice Cavallotti and Silvio Pellico. Among international plays were those by Dumas, Hugo, Sardou, Zola, and Ibsen. Among the most prolific radical playwrights of the Little Italies were Alessandro Sisca (alias Riccardo Cordiferro), Arturo Giovannitti, Vincenzo Vacirca, Alberico Molinari, and Ludovico Caminita.

[15] The importance of dramatic groups in the culture of the Italian anarchists is noted by Paul Avrich in his *Sacco and Vanzetti: The Anarchist Background* (Princeton: Princeton University Press, 1991), 55.

their daily life.[16] But, as in the case of the other radical theatres, the *sovversivi*'s stage was also seen as an important shaper of public opinion and a crucial catalyst in the making of social consciousness.[17] Its primary function was to awake the political and social consciousness of the spectators. Hence most of the performances were designed as morality plays with dialogs and situations which Italian American workers could easily understand and characters with whom they could easily identify. Plots dealt essentially with themes of social awareness. They were "problem" plays, which focused on general social issues and usually contained a strong indictment of capitalism. But the subject matter was drawn from distinct Italian events or problems peculiar to the Italian American community. For example, Fascism or the *padrone*-system were distinctive themes of the Italian American radical stage.[18]

Financial reports published in the Italian American radical press indicate that radical performances were very successful, collecting between thirty and fifty dollars a night. Since admission cost between five to ten cents and was usually free to children and women, we can estimate that about 500 people, and sometimes as many as 1,000 people, typically attended these performances.

Other cultural activities sponsored by radical groups, such as dances, picnics or public lectures also drew large audiences, often much larger than union or party meetings. The *New York Times* for example, noted that the Bresci group of East Harlem, New York (so called in honor of Gaetano Bresci, the anarchist who assassinated King Vittorio Emmanuele in 1900) organized lectures regularly on Sunday that "drew as many as 150 people."[19] Similarly, Italian language radical newspapers often commented on the overwhelming success of the special events (or *serate speciali* as they were called in Italian) sponsored by radical groups. As early as 1894, the anarchist publication *Il Grido degli Oppressi*, for example, reported that

---

[16] Cf. Maxine Schwartz Seller, "Introduction" to *Ethnic Theatre in the United States* (Westport, CT: Greenwood Press, 1983), 3-17.

[17] See Edna Nahshon, *Yiddish Proletarian Theatre, The Arts and Politics of the Artef, 1925-1940* (Westport, CT: Greenwood Press, 1998); Colette Hyman, *Workers' Theatre and the American Labor Movement* (Philadelphia: Temple University Press, 1997).

[18] Italians dealt with Fascism since 1922, whereas Americans and other ethnic groups did not concern themselves with Fascism until the Popular Front.

[19] "Bomb Sleuth Lived with Anarchists," *New York Times*, March 3, 1915, 6.

the *Serata di famiglia* they had helped organize had attracted 400 Italians and lasted until 4:00AM.[20]

It was often through these cultural venues that radical leaders most successfully expressed and carried their political ideology beyond the confines of the workplace. While it is impossible to know whether plays effectively radicalized the workers who attended them, there is evidence that in some cases they did help recruit new members. For example, Joseph Moro, a shoemaker, converted to anarchism overnight after seeing an anarchist performance. He arrived in the United States in 1911, at the age of sixteen, and settled in Stoneham, Massachusetts. Raised within a devout Catholic milieu, Moro was initially a very religious boy, a "mystic" as he put it. But in 1912 he attended a picnic organized by Italian anarchists near Wakefield, Massachusetts. "I found the place just in time to see *Calendimaggio*, a play by Pietro Gori," he recalled. "I was deeply moved. It inspired me so much that in twenty-four hours I gave up all my religion, all my former beliefs and started to read anarchist literature." From then on, he worked closely with anarchist groups and served as the last secretary of the Sacco-Vanzetti Defense Committee.[21]

Regrettably, most radical scripts have been entirely lost. However, a few important plays can be found in specialized archival collections as well as in the pages of radical newspapers, which frequently published entire one-act plays or installments of social dramas. For example the literary magazine *Il Fuoco* (1914-1915) directed by Arturo Giovannitti and Onorio Ruotolo, featured a dramatic skit in almost every issue.[22] These

---

[20] *Il Grido degli Oppressi*, November 30, 1894.

[21] Paul Avrich, *Anarchist Voices: An Oral History of Anarchism in America* (Edinburgh: AK Press, 2005; first published in 1995), 113.

[22] For example: Silvio Picchianti, "Tribunali domestici," November 15, 1914, 12-14; F. Simeotti "L'alcova ardente," December 1, 1914, 14-16; G. Sterni "Convegno," December 13, 1914, 20-21; " La morte in agguato," January 1, 1915, 14-16, "La guerra," February 1, 1915, 13-15, and "Don Luca Sperante," October 15, 1914, 12-13 all by Ario Flamma. *Il Fuoco* also published several plays by Arturo Giovannitti. *Il Fuoco* is available in microfilm at the New York Public Library. For a discussion of these plays see Marcella Bencivenni, "A Magazine of Art and Politics: The Experience of *Il Fuoco*, 1914-15," *The Italian American Review* (Spring/Summer 2001): 57-84. A few original plays can also be found in *Il Proletario*. See for example "Le vittime del capitalism," author unknown, June 12, 1920 and Angelo Ciccarelli, "Orgoglio Funesto," published in installments from June 17 to November 6, 1937. This play was performed on February 20, 1938 at Arlington Hall in New York City. For a fuller discussion of Italian immigrant radical theater see Chapter 4 of my *Italian Immigrant Radical Culture*.

plays offer a unique opportunity to peek into the world of working-class *divertimenti*—entertainments—and study the interaction of cultural, political, and recreational activities.

Following Italian radicals through their own communities, institutions, and activities allows us, in the words of Ardis Cameron, "to tunnel beneath the wall that has traditionally separated the public and private lives of workers," and develop "an alternative notion of politics—one developed relationally . . . and rooted in the material reality of everyday life."[23]

To fully understand the world of Italian immigrant radicalism we must study, as cultural and social historians have long urged, not only the work place and the political space but also the social space—those autonomous spheres of cultural interaction and exchange through which people experienced radicalism. We must look at workers' thoughts, attitudes and feelings, re-create their consciousness, historicize their experiences and explore the forms of everyday life through which they voiced their ideas. We must, in other words, ask not only where and why class consciousness is raised, but how.[24] Only viewed in this way, in the myriad intersections of culture and politics, can we finally give true justice to the multifaceted world of Italian American radicalism, a world that as Spencer M. Di Scala noted, "may have been 'lost' but not forsaken."[25]

In fact, one could say, practically nothing has remained of the *sovversivi*'s political tradition in the United States. Along with much of the American Left, Italian American radicalism, at least in the political sense of a counter-ideology to capitalism, vanished after the Second World War. But, given its earlier vibrancy and richness, how do we explain its loss?

The question, to be fair, does not concern exclusively Italian Americans but could be related in many ways, as Donna Gabaccia also noted, to a larger question that German sociologist Werner Sombart raised more than a century ago: why is there no socialism in the United States?[26] Why

---

[23] Ardis Cameron, *Radicals of the Worst Sort: Laboring Women in Lawrence, Massachusetts, 1860-1912* (Urbana: University of Illinois Press, 1995), 4-5.

[24] Ibid., 4.

[25] "Foreword" to Cannistraro and Meyer, *The Lost World of Italian American Radicalism,* viii.

[26] Werner Sombart's article *Why Is There No Socialism in the United States,* was first published in 1908 but appeared in English in its entirety only in 1976 (London: Macmillan Press). See also Seymour Martin Lipset and Gary Marks, eds., *It Didn't Happen Here: Why Socialism Failed in the United States* (New York: W.W. Norton, 2000).

did the most capitalist nation of all fail to produce a socialist tradition or a lasting communist party as in modern Europe? Or, seen from a comparative perspective, why was the radical tradition lost among Italian Americans, but not in Italy, or among Italians in other parts of the world, such as France, Germany or Argentina?[27]

As Eric Foner pointed out in 1984, what must be explained is not so much why there is no socialism in America (because, as many have documented, there was in fact socialism), but why it rose and fell. Posed this way, the question, suggests Foner, requires that we "historicize" the problem of American socialism.[28]

As the *sovversivi*'s story suggests, Italian immigrants were not conservative at arrival. On the contrary, they came with a wide range of radical experiences, ideas, and traditions, and created vibrant radical communities throughout the United States. But specific historical conditions and circumstances, both internal and external to the movement, redefined their political ideas, transforming, and eventually destroying, Italian immigrant radicalism.

One factor was certainly the enormous diversity and sectarian orientation of the movement. Not only was the Italian immigrant Left, as the Left in general, sharply divided ideologically among anarchists, socialists, syndicalists, communists, and social democrats, but members within each group constantly argued with one another, as in the case, for example, of the organizational and anti-organizational anarchists, or the reformist and revolutionary socialists.[29] Although a few radical leaders like Giovannitti and Tresca managed to transcend these ideological divisions and forge broader alliances, the *sovversivi* were never really able to achieve unity. Rather than channelling their militancy towards political purposes, they wasted energy and time fighting endlessly over theoretical issues and the "correct" methods of struggle. In doing so, they succumbed to the kind of ideological rigidity that sabotaged other leftist movements, hin-

---

[27] Donna Gabaccia, "Lost and Found: Italian American Radicalism in Global Perspective," in Cannistraro and Meyer, eds., *The Lost World of Italian American Radicalism*, 315.

[28] Eric Foner, "Why is there no Socialism in the United States," *History Workshop*, 17 (Spring 1984), 57-80.

[29] See Nunzio Pernicone, "War among the Italian Anarchists: The Galleanisti's Campaign against Carlo Tresca," in Cannistraro and Meyer, eds., *The Lost World of Italian American Radicalism*, 77-97.

dering them from effectively challenging the hegemony of bourgeois culture.[30]

An even deeper wound inflicted on the Italian immigrant Left was what the late Rudolph Vecoli described as the "fascistization" of the Little Italies.[31] As Cannistraro and other scholars have documented, Fascism gained considerable support among Italians in the United States. The first *fascio*, or fascist organization, was founded in New York City as early as 1921. Four years later, as the *fasci* began to multiply, Mussolini created the Fascist League of North America (AFANA) to coordinate and supervise their activities. Although he was forced to disband AFANA in 1929, he was able to establish a strong power base for his propaganda through the support of the Catholic clergy, the Italian Consulate, and, especially, the local business and political elite, the so-called *prominenti*, who controlled the Italian language media and the major institutions of the immigrant community.[32]

Although in the estimate of antifascist historian Gaetano Salvemini only 5% of Italian Americans were true Fascists, thousands of them looked at Mussolini as a source of ethnic pride.[33] Fascist rhetoric of restoring Italy's greatness and Mussolini's grandiose image—as a living symbol of the presumed moral, political and economic regeneration of Italy—effectively fueled the patriotic sentiments of Italian Americans. Particularly, Mussolini's emphasis on "Old World" values with the famous slogan: *"la religione, la patria e la famiglia"* (religion, fatherland and family) suc-

---

[30] See Daniel Bell, *Marxian Socialism in the United States* (Princeton: Princeton University Press, 1967) and James Weinstein, *The Decline of Socialism in America* (New York: Knopf, 1967).

[31] See Rudolph Vecoli, "The Making and Un-making of the Italian American Working Class," in Cannistraro and Meyer, eds., *The Lost World of Italian American Radicalism*, 51-75.

[32] On Italian Americans and Fascism see John P. Diggins, *Mussolini and Fascism: The View from America* (Princeton: Princeton University Press, 1972); Philip V. Cannistraro, "Per una storia dei fasci negli Stati Uniti," *Storia Contemporanea* 6 (December 1995): 1061-1145; Cannistraro, "Fascism and Italian Americans," in Silvio M. Tomasi, ed., *Perspectives in Italian Immigration and Ethnicity* (New York: Center for Migration Studies, 1977); Cannistraro, *Blackshirts in Little Italy* (West Lafayette: Bordighera, 2000); Nunzio Pernicone, *Carlo Tresca: Portrait of a Rebel* (New York: Palgrave, 2005), 127-134; Daria Bicocchi Frezza, "Propaganda fascista e comunità italiane in USA: La Casa Italiana della Columbia University," *Studi Storici* (October/November 1970): 661-97; and Charles Fama, "Fascist Propaganda in the United States," *La Parola del Popolo* (December 1958-Janaury 1959), 91-92.

[33] Gaetano Salvemini, *Italian Fascist Activities in the United States*, edited with an introduction by Philip Cannistraro (New York: Center for Migration Studies, 1977), 244-45.

cessfully played upon Italian immigrants' nostalgic nationalism and fears of family and community disintegration resulting from Americanization and generational conflict.

This emergent ethnic nationalism powerfully undermined the class internationalism and radical militancy of the early period and insinuated racial and ethnic prejudices in the minds of many Italian Americans.[34] Interestingly, however, Italian immigrants in other parts of the world, such as France, Belgium, and Argentina, did not support Fascism. As comparative studies have evidenced, it was the peculiar conditions of Italians in the United States—particularly the persistent prejudices and discrimination they encountered—that made them vulnerable to Fascism.[35]

Italian American radicalism was also eroded by external forces, particularly state repression. Along with the rest of the American Left, the Italian radical movement in the United States was seriously crippled by the Red Scare of 1919—the anti-radical hysteria that gripped the United States after the triumph of the Russian Revolution. Radical organizations were dismantled, newspapers suppressed, and thousands of militants arrested and sentenced to long term prison sentences under draconian laws like the Espionage Act (1917) and the Sedition Act (1918). Italian anarchists were primary targets of this anti-radical crusade. Luigi Galleani, the charismatic and influential leader of the organizational anarchists was indicted and deported in 1919 along with many dedicated followers. Among those caught in the FBI roundups were the anarchists Sacco and Vanzetti, who were arrested in 1920 on questionable charges of robbery and murder. Their controversial trial and consequent execution in 1927 had most certainly a demoralizing effect on Italian Americans, pressuring them to distance themselves from "un-American" radical values.

---

[34] Prior to Fascism, Italian Americans had strongly condemned racial bigotry and lynching. Mussolini's war on Ethiopia deeply influenced the racial attitudes of Italian Americans. Similarly the anti-Semitic laws enacted by the Fascist regime in 1938 had implications for Italian American relations with Jews. Cf. Vecoli, " The Making and Un-Making of the Italian American Working Class."

[35] See for example Pietro Rinaldi Fanesi, "Italian Antifascism and the Garibaldine Tradition in Latin America," and Antonio Bachelloni, "Antifascist Resistance in France from the 'Phony War' to Liberation: Identities and Destinies in Question," both in Donna Gabaccia and Fraser Ottanelli, eds., *Italian Workers of the World: Labor Migration and the Formation of Multiethnic States* (Urbana: University of Illinois Press, 2001), 163-77 and 214-31, respectively.

The Cold War and its attendant political repression completed the purge of radicalism from Italian American communities and American society at large. In his famous speech of March 1947, President Truman insisted that freedom was threatened by communism and that the United States had a "duty" to defend the world from the Soviet influence. Nine days later, he issued an executive order for interrogations to verify the patriotism and loyalty of federal employees, and the House Committee on Un-American Activities began its investigations of communist influence on the entertainment industry.

More pervasive than the Red Scare that followed the Great War, the repression of the 1950s stretched out for many years, permanently destroying whatever was left of radical organizations and causing another controversial trial and execution: that of Ethel and Julius Rosenberg in 1953. [36] Many Italian radicals in the United States were deported. Anarchist Armando Borghi was repatriated in 1945, and so was communist Michele (Mike) Salerno, editor of *L'Unità Operaia* and *L'Unità del Popolo*, in 1950.[37] Carl Marzani, an important but neglected figure of the Italian American Left was also arrested in 1947 and sentenced to thirty-two months in jail as a former communist, becoming in his own words "the first victim of McCarthyism."[38]

The radical seed that the *sovversivi* had planted at the beginning of the twentieth century and had kept alive for four decades was finally and effectively eradicated with disastrous consequences for the future of Italian American, and American, radical politics. Like the Sacco and Vanzetti case in the 1920s, the Red Scare of the 1950s succeeded in equating Americanism with anti-communism and promoting political conservatism and consensus. Implying the superiority of American culture, the Truman Doctrine encouraged children of old immigrants to Americanize as quickly as possible. Italian Americans increasingly saw their parents' ways as shameful and began to distance themselves from their radical past, fearing the stigma that marked those who displayed radical sympathies.[39]

---

[36] For an overview of the Cold War era see Howard Zinn, *Post-War America: 1945-1971* (Indianapolis: Bobbs-Merrill, 1973) and Melvyn Leffler, *A Preponderance of Power: National Security, The Truman Administration, and the Cold War* (Stanford: Stanford University Press, 1992).

[37] See Eric Salerno, *Rossi a Manhattan* (Rome: Quiritta, 2001).

[38] Cited in Gerald Meyer, "Italian Americans and the American Communist Party," in Cannistraro and Meyer, eds., *The Lost World of Italian American Radicalism*, 217.

[39] Vecoli, "The Making and Un-Making of the Italian American Working Class," 63-64.

The psychological impact of the Red Scares on the minds of Italian Americans and other immigrants has yet to be established. There is no doubt however that it successfully silenced the political opposition, forcing many to erase their radical history. In fact as Cannistraro and Meyer wrote in their introduction, "For most Italian Americans," the experiences of grandparents and parents are replete with deafening silences that are the product in part of fears and taboos that drove many first-generation immigrants to bury aspects of their past that seemed to make them somehow too Italian and not sufficiently American." Far from atypical, Cammella's story, they noted, remains a powerful reminder of immigrants' reluctance to discuss their radical past.[40]

For instance, Cannistraro discovered by accident that his apparently conservative grandfather had attended communist meetings in the Bronx and participated in anti-Fascist demonstrations in the 1940s after Jennifer Guglielmo and Gerald Meyer found his grandfather's name among the contributors and readers of the communist paper *L'Unità del Popolo*.[41]

Years ago, while I was conducting my doctoral research, I found among the pages of the syndicalist newspaper *Il proletario* the text of a famous Italian communist song entitled *Bandiera Rossa* (Red Flag). After I improvised the tune of the song at a small party at Cannistraro's house, an Italian American woman of about eighty years old told me that the music reminded her of a song her mother used to sing. However, as soon as I told her what the song was about, horrified she exclaimed: "Oh no, then I made a mistake. . . . There are no Commies in my family!" Clearly, as Donna Gabaccia commented, Americanism and radicalism had become incompatible: immigrants and radicals "try as they may, could not simultaneously be good leftists and good Americans."[42]

The political rupture between generations, however, can also be attributed, as Vecoli and Pernicone suggest, to distinctive Italian family dynamics. Family roles in the traditional Italian family were notoriously rigid. Women were expected to stay home and fulfill their roles as mothers and wives without interfering with the world of politics which was re-

---

[40] Cannistraro and Meyer, "Italian American Radicalism: An Interpretative History," 2. See also Janet Zandy, *Hands, Physical Labor, Class, and Cultural Work* (New Brunswick: Rutgers University Press, 2004, 56

[41] Cited in Cannistraro and Meyer, eds., *The Lost World*, endnote n. 3, 32-33.

[42] Gabaccia, "Lost and Found: Italian American Radicalism in Global Perspective," in Cannistraro and Meyer, eds., *The Lost World of Italian American Radicalism*, 321.

garded as a male sphere. Even though many women challenged these norms, and even though, at least in theory, radical men condemned gender oppression, radicalism produced little change in the gendered divisions of the Italian American family. Italian immigrant children continued to be raised mostly by their mothers, while their fathers spent little time at home, and, when home, rarely talked about politics. Alienated by their fathers' world, they became consequently unable to absorb their radical ideas.[44]

Economic advancement was another important factor that distanced Italian Americans from their radical past. New occupational opportunities created by the Second World War favored social mobility, expanding the Italian American middle class and led growing numbers of them to identify their interests with the status quo. In the post-World War II period Italian Americans began to move out of the old working class neighborhoods into gentrified suburbs, and increasingly became more conservative and reactionary.[45]

However, as the last section of *The Lost World of Italian American Radicalism* indicates, traces of Italian American radicalism can be found in the individual struggles of some exceptional figures within the civil rights movement, the women's liberation movement, and, more recently, in the movement for gay and lesbian rights. This is the case for example of Father James Groppi, the civil rights leader of Milwaukee, who fused his Christian faith with a leftist commitment to social justice and equality; or Mario Savio, a significant figure of the New Left and the Free Speech Movement of the 1960s, who was expelled by his university and sentenced to four months of prison for his political activism.[46] Perhaps more strongly, an Italian American radical tradition survives today in the work of novelists and artists who have explored new "radical" themes such as

---

[44] Cf. Vecoli, "The Making and Un-Making of the Italian American Working Class," 64, and Nunzio Pernicone, "Italian Immigrant Radicalism in New York City," in Philip V. Cannistraro, ed., *The Italians of New York* (NY: New York Historical Society, 1999), 88.

[45] See Richard Alba, *Italian Americans into the Twilight of Ethnicity* (Englewood Cliffs, NJ: Prentice Hall, 1985).

[46] See Jackie Di Salvo, "Father James E. Groppi (1930-1985): The Militant Humility of a Civil Rights Activist," and Gil Fagiani, "Mario Savio: Resurrecting an Italian American Radical," in Cannistraro and Meyer, eds., *The Lost World of Italian American Radicalism*, 229-244 and 245-252, respectively.

generational conflict, gender oppression and homosexuality.[47] But this brand of radicalism belongs more to the liberal currents of the United States, than the anti-capitalist politics of the early Italian immigrant Left.

As Donna Gabaccia noted, one perhaps should talk about a transformation or Americanization of Italian American radicalism, rather than its irreversible demise. One can notice a shift from a radicalism "made-in-Italy" intended as a collective political struggle aiming at a fundamental transformation of capitalism, to a radicalism defined by racial, gender, and ethnic identity, connected to personal transformation and consciousness.

This shift also illustrates the evolution of left politics in the United States from the anti-capitalist struggle of the early twentieth century to the personal politics of today. Significantly, as Gabaccia pointed out, this connection of the personal and the political is what also distinguishes American studies of radicalism from their counterparts in other nations. While in the United States radicalism is more fluid, linked to personal identity politics rather than class politics, in Italy and Europe the term continues to be used to identify people and movements committed to a transformation of capitalism.[48]

Even though Italian American political radicalism has disappeared, the radical experience, as discussed earlier, has become a central frame of reference and a distinctive subfield of Italian American history. There are also signs that Italian Americans have begun to rediscover and take interest in their radical past. Indeed, there is much in that history that is admirable, inspiring, and noble. The *sovversivi* put forward a distinctive worldview centered on universalism, solidarity, social justice and equality. In a time in which consumerism, individualism, fundamentalism and anti-immigration feelings are rampant, the *sovversivi*'s struggle and dream for a better world can offer refreshing hope. Indeed, some of the issues that radicals were sorting out in the first half of the twentieth cen-

---

[47] Examples of a continuing radical tradition among Italian Americans are progressive activists and politicians such as John Pastore, Mario Cuomo, Mario DiSalvio and Peter Rodino, or novelists such as Pietro Di Donato, Jerre Mangione, Carl Marzani and Diane Di Prima. See the essays by Fred Gardaphe, Julia Lisella, Mary Jo Bona and Edvige Giunta in Cannistraro and Meyer, eds., *The Lost World of Italian American Radicalism*.

[48] Donna Gabaccia, "Lost and Found: Italian American Radicalism in Global Perspective," in Cannistraro and Meyer, eds., *The Lost World of Italian American Radicalism*, 318.

tury—unorganized labor, increasing social inequality, economic insecurity, class, ethnic and racial oppression—have hardly been settled.

A recovery of the "lost world of Italian American radicalism" means much more than correcting the distortions of earlier historiography and breaking the silences of a past generation of activists; it represents a challenge to the dominant neoliberal politics and the rampant nativist sentiments of our times. Italian Americans in particular, as Rudolph Vecoli suggested, need to learn from this revolutionary legacy to free themselves "from an apologetic ethnicity that is too much dominated by a reactionary, chauvinist and racist ideology."[49]

---

[49] Vecoli, "The Making and Un-making of the Italian American Working Class," in Cannistraro and Meyer, eds., *The Lost World of Italian American Radicalism*, 64.

New Directions in Italian and Italian-American History: A Conference in Honor of Philip Cannistraro

Saturday, November, 5, 2011

John D. Calandra Italian American Institute

25 West 43rd Street 17th Floor, New York City (212) 642-2094

Keynote, 10-11 AM

Emilio Gentile, University of Rome, La Sapienza
"Fabbrica del consenso o fabbrica del potere? Redefining Fascism and Totalitarianism"

New Directions in Italian-American History, 11:15 AM-12:30 PM

Chair: Gerald Meyer, Hostos Community College, CUNY
Charles Killinger, University of Central Florida, "Italian Antifascist Exiles and the Italian-American Community: Renato Poggioli and Gaetano Salvemini as Case Studies"
Marcella Bencivenni, Hostos Community College, CUNY, "Re-examining Italian-American Radical History Through the Lens of Culture"
Peter Vellon, Queens College, CUNY, "'The humiliation of being treated like Negroes': The Italian-American Education in Matters of Race"

New Directions in Italian History, I, 2:15-3:30 PM

Chair: Emily Braun, Hunter College & The Graduate Center, CUNY
Paul Corner, University of Siena, "Factories and their Products: A Comment on Phil Cannistraro's *La fabbrica del consenso*"
Ernest Ialongo, Hostos Community College, CUNY, "The Calculated Compromise: F.T. Marinetti and Fascism in the Twenties"

William Adams, Hunter College, CUNY, "The Politica dei ponti in the Republic of Salò"

New Directions in Italian History, II, 3:45-5:00 PM

Chair: John Davis, University of Connecticut

Marta Petrusewicz, University of Calabria, "Fin-de-siècle Rome: A Republic of Collectors"

Stanislao Pugliese, Hofstra University, "Dancing on a Volcano: Attempting a Popular History of Naples"

David Aliano, College of Mount Saint Vincent, "Re-imagining the Nation: Italian National Narratives Abroad (1922-1945)"

PARTICIPANTS

An asterix by a name represents a contributor to this volume as well.

*WILLIAM ADAMS graduated from UCLA with a B.A. in English before attending the CUNY Graduate Center, where he earned a Ph.D. in Modern European History. His dissertation, "Mussolini and Intellectuals in the Republic of Salò, 1943-1945," was conceived and partially written under the supervision of Philip Cannistraro. He teaches as an adjunct assistant professor at Hunter College, and is co-organizer of "New Directions in Italian and Italian-American History."

DAVID ALIANO is Assistant Professor of History and Modern Languages and Literatures at the College of Mount Saint Vincent. He earned his Ph.D. in Modern European and Latin American History at the Graduate Center of the City University of New York in 2008. He earned a Master of Philosophy in History at the CUNY Graduate Center in 2005 and received his Bachelor of the Arts Degree in History and Italian at Fordham University in 2000. He has published peer-reviewed articles in the *Ethnic Studies Review* (2010), *French Colonial History* (2008), *Estudios Interdisciplinarios de America Latina y el Caribe* (2006), and *Altreitalie* (2005). He is the author of *Mussolini's National Project in Argentina* (Fairleigh Dickinson University Press, 2012).

*MARCELLA BENCIVENNI is Assistant Professor of History at Hostos Community College of the City University of New York. She is the author of *Italian Immigrant Radical Culture: The Idealism of the Sovversivi in the United States, 1890-1940* (New York University Press, 2011), and co-editor with Ron Hayduk of *Radical Perspectives on Immigration*, a special issue of the journal *Socialism and Democracy* (November 2008), of which she is a board member. She has also written numerous articles about American labor, immigration and Italian-American history and presented her research at national and international conferences. She is currently completing an essay on radical production and consumption for a book edited by Simone Cinotto, *All Things Italian: Consumer Culture in Italian American History* (under contract with Fordham University Press) and is also starting a new project on the Triangle Fire in Italian American history and memory.

EMILY BRAUN is Distinguished Professor, Hunter College and the Graduate Center, CUNY. She has written extensively on twentieth century Italian art and Fascist culture, including her book, *Mario Sironi and Italian Modernism: Art and Politics under Fascism* (Cambridge University Press, 2000) and most recently, "The

Modernity of Tradition: The Fine Arts in Fascist Italy 1919-1929," in *Reinterpreting the Past*, ed. Irena Kossowska (Warsaw: Polish Academy of Sciences, 2011). Her co-authored book, *The Power of Conversation: Jewish Women and their Salons* (Yale University Press, 2005) won the National Jewish Book Award. For the last four years she has also been the Chair of the Art History Program, and Deputy Chair of the Department of Art and Art History at Hunter College. Her current research is on Italian art and culture of the immediate post-war era.

*PAUL CORNER is Professor of European History at the University of Siena and Director of the Euromasters programme. He has been the Director of the Centre for the Advanced Study of Italian Society, University of Reading (UK), and has been a fellow or visiting professor at the British Academy, European University Institute, Paul Nitz School for Advanced International Studies at the Johns Hopkins Bologna Center, the Italian Academy for Advanced Studies at Columbia University, the Remarque Institute at New York University, and was the Fondazione Monte dei Paschi di Siena Fellow at St. Antony's College, Oxford. In 2005 he was elected Member of Senior Common Room, St Antony's College, Oxford. He is a member of the editorial boards of *The Italianist*, and *The Journal of Modern Italian Studies*. Recent publications include his edited volume *Popular Opinion in Totalitarian Regimes. Fascism, Nazism, Communism* (Oxford, 2009; Laterza, 2012) and his *The Party and the People: Why Italian Fascism Failed* (Oxford, 2012; Laterza, 2013).

JOHN DAVIS holds the Emiliana Pasca Noether Chair in Modern Italian History at the University of Connecticut and is Editor of the *Journal of Modern Italian Studies*. A John Simon Guggenheim Fellow, his work on modern Italian history has been recognized by the award of the Serena Medal of the British Academy and the International Galileo Galilei Prize. A Resident of the American Academy in Rome, a Fellow of the Royal Historical Society (London) and a member of the academic board of the *Istituto Italiano per gli Studi Filosofici*, he has taught and lectured at numerous universities in Italy and Europe as well as the USA. He is general editor of the seven-volume *Oxford Short History of Italy* (Oxford, 2000-2006) and has edited many collective volumes, including *Italy and America 1943-4* (Naples, 1997). Major recent publications include *Naples and Napoleon. Southern Italy in the Age of the European Revolutions* (Oxford, 2006), which won the Howard and Helen Marraro Prize of the American Historical Association for the best book on Italy in any period (2007), the *Premio Internazionale Sele d'Oro* and the Literary Award of the International Napoleonic Society. His latest book, *The Jews of San Nicandro*, is published by Yale University Press (2010).

*EMILIO GENTILE is Professor of History at the University of Rome, La Sapienza, and has been visiting professor in Australia, France and the United States. In 2003 he received the Hans Sigrist Prize from the University of Berne for his work on the religious nature of politics. His research interests include Fascism, nationalism, Futurism, the Great War, totalitarianism, the sacralization of politics and American civil religion. His works that have been translated into English, as well as the major foreign languages, include: *The Sacralization of Politics in Fascist Italy* (Harvard, 1996), *The Struggle for Modernity: Nationalism, Futurism, and Fascism* (Praeger, 2003), *Fascist Ideology* (Enigma Books, 2005), *Politics as Religion* (Princeton, 2006), *God's Democracy: American Religion after September 11* (Praeger, 2008), *La Grande Italia. The Myth of the Nation in the 20th Century* (Wisconsin, 2009).

*ERNEST IALONGO is Assistant Professor of History at Hostos Community College in The City University of New York. He recently published "Filippo Tommaso Marinetti: The Artist and his Politics" in *Futurismo: Impact and Legacy* (New York, 2011), and has presented his work at a number of venues in America and Europe. In 2011 he organized the following panels, on which he also presented his work: "Reconsidering Futurism" at the American Historical Association conference, and "The Inconvenient Politics of Modern European Artists" at the Modernist Studies Association conference. He is the co-organizer of "New Directions in Italian and Italian-American History." He is currently completing a book that analyzes Marinetti's politics from Liberal to Fascist Italy (1909-1944).

*CHARLES KILLINGER is Patricia Warren Endowed Chair and Emeritus at Valencia College and Adjunct and Graduate Professor of History at the University of Central Florida. Among his publications are numerous articles and reviews and several books, including a biography of Gaetano Salvemini and a History of Italy. His chapter in an anthology on Renato Poggioli is due for publication in 2012.

*GERALD MEYER is a founding member of the faculty of Hostos Community College (CUNY). He is the author of *Vito Marcantonio: Radical Politician, 1902-1954* (which is in its fourth printing) and with Philip Cannistraro, co-editor of *The Lost World of Italian American Radicalism*. He has published over sixty articles and reviews on a wide range of subjects including the intersection of radicalism and immigrants, culture and the Left, and the history of the Communist Party. Gerald Meyer is on the editorial boards of *Socialism and Democracy* and *Science & Society*, appears in documentaries, he reviews manuscripts for publication, and lectures widely.

MARTA PETRUSEWICZ has studied and worked in Poland, Italy, France and the United States and currently teaches Modern European History at the Università della Calabria. She is the author, among others, of *Latifundium: Moral Economy and Material Life in a 19th-Century Periphery; Un sogno irlandese: la storia di Constance Markiewicz comandante dell'IRA* and *Come il Meridione divenne Questione: rappresentazioni del Sud prima e dopo il 1848*, and the editor, with Jane Schneider and Peter Schneider of *Sud: conoscere, capire, cambiare*. She is currently writing a comparative history of the European peripheries in the 19th century.

*STANISLAO PUGLIESE is professor of modern European history and the Queensboro Unico Distinguished Professor of Italian and Italian American Studies at Hofstra University. In 2005 he was named Teacher of the Year by the Association of Italian American Educators. Dr. Pugliese is a former research fellow at the Italian Academy for Advanced Studies at Columbia University, the United States Holocaust Memorial Museum, Oxford University and Harvard University. A specialist on the Italian anti-fascist Resistance and Italian Jews, he is the author, editor or translator of a dozen books on Italian and Italian American history. He is the editor of the Italian and Italian American Studies series published by Palgrave Macmillan. In 2009, Farrar, Straus & Giroux published his book, *Bitter Spring: A Life of Ignazio Silone*. He is currently working on a new book, tentatively titled *Dancing on a Volcano: A Cultural History of Naples*.

PETER G. VELLON is Assistant Professor of History at Queens College where he teaches courses on Italian American history, race and ethnicity, immigration, and the U.S. war in Vietnam. His book '*America is a White Nation': The Italian Language Press in New York City and the Making of Race, 1886-1919* will be published by New York University Press in its *Culture, Labor, History* series. He contributed an essay to the recently published compilation, *Anti-Italianism: Essays on a Prejudice*, edited by William J. Connell and Fred Gardaphé, and will co-edit the American Italian Historical Association's 2010 Conference Proceedings, *Advocacy and Activism: Italian Heritage and Cultural Change*. In addition, he has published articles in the *Italian American Review* and has presented papers at many major historical conferences, including the American Historical Association's annual conference, as well as the yearly conference of the American Italian Historical Association.

INDEX

Marinetti, Filippo Tommaso, v, 4, 27, 28, 29, 30, 31, 32, 33, 34, 35, 36, 37, 38, 39, 120, 124
Marzani, Carl, 105, 115, 118
Matteotti, Giacomo, 32, 67
Mazzini, 62, 66, 68, 69, 70, 71, 73, 76
McDonald, Michael P., 60
Meyer, Gerald, v, 3, 5, 77, 89, 90, 92, 93, 94, 95, 96, 97, 98, 99, 101, 102, 104, 111, 112, 113, 115, 116, 117, 118, 119, 120, 124
Michelangelo, 69
Moro, Joseph, 110
Mosse, George L., 13
Mussolini, Benito, 1, 2, 5, 7, 8, 14, 15, 16, 17, 19, 20, 23, 24, 28, 29, 30, 32, 33, 34, 35, 36, 38, 39, 40, 41, 42, 43, 44, 45, 46, 47, 48, 49, 59, 71, 72, 75, 105, 113, 114, 122

Origo, Iris, 58
Ottanelli, Fraser, 105, 114

Pacciardi, Randolfo, 69, 70, 73, 75
Parson, Talcott, 53
Pavolini, Alessandro, 44, 45
Pernicone, Nunzio, 94, 104, 105
Petrusewicz, Marta, vii, 3, 4, 121, 124
Pettinato, Concetto, 47, 48
Pini, Giorgio, 45, 46, 47
Poggioli, Renato, v, 4, 5, 65, 66, 67, 68, 69, 70, 71, 72, 73, 74, 75, 76, 120, 124
Proudhon, Pierre-Joseph, 55
Pugliese, Stanislao G., v, 4, 5, 50, 61, 121, 125

Rampa Rossi, Franco, 35, 36
Rapisardi, Mario, 107
Roosevelt, Franklin Delano, 59, 83, 89, 90, 91, 95
Rosselli, Carlo, 10, 61

Salerno, Michele, 40, 68, 75, 100, 115
Salomone, A. Wlliam, 104
Salvemini, Gaetano, v, 5, 6, 10, 65, 66, 67, 68, 69, 70, 71, 72, 73, 74, 75, 76, 113, 114, 120, 124

Sarfatti, Margherita, 2, 7, 30
Savio, Mario, 118
Silone, Darina, 52
Silone, Ignazio, v, 5, 50, 51, 52, 53, 54, 55, 56, 57, 58, 59, 60, 61, 62, 63, 64, 125
Sironi, Mario, 35, 122
Smith, Alfred E., 66, 67, 68, 90, 95
Soffici, Ardengo, 36, 37
Spada, Paolo, 51
Spina, Pietro, 51, 56, 59, 60, 62
Stevenson, Adlai, 59
Sturzo, Luigi, 10, 69, 75
Sullivan, Brian R., 2, 30

Tamburri, Anthony Julian, vii, viii, 3, 98, 101
Teoli, Cammella, 102, 103
Togliatti, Palmiro, 10
Tranquilli, Secondino, 50
Tresca, Carlo, 100, 103, 105, 112, 113

Ulam, Adam, 68, 76

Vecoli, Rudolph, 77, 88, 89, 92, 101, 105, 113, 114, 116, 117, 119
Vellon, Peter, vii, 3, 4, 120, 125
Vico, Giambattista, 52
von Hofmannsthal, Hugo, 53
von Rahn, Rudolf, 44

Weil, Simone, 51

www.ingramcontent.com/pod-product-compliance
Lightning Source LLC
Chambersburg PA
CBHW081408270326
41931CB00016B/3417